OTHER BOOKS BY BARBARA MOON

www.lulu.com/barbaramoon   www.amazon.com

Handbook to Joy-Filled Parenting

Workbook for Handbook to Joy-Filled Parenting

Workbook and Guide for Hinds' Feet on High Places

Leader's Guide for Hinds' Feet on High Places'

Workbook and Guide for The Rest of the Gospel

Leader's Guide for The Rest of the Gospel

The Lost Dome of Atron-Book One

The Genesis of Atron-Book Two

The Redemption of Atron-Book Three

Jewels for My Journey

Jesus Never Fails

The Craziosity Twins

Joy-Filled Relationships

by

Barbara Moon

TABLE OF CONTENTS

THANKS

I want to thank Juli May for her suggestion to make a book out of the brain science chapters in the *Handbook to Joy-Filled Parenting*[1] and to add in all the handouts I've made from THRIVE material. It has been very rewarding to pass on what I have learned from the THRIVE Conferences.

I also want to thank all the gals who have been with me in various small groups as we have gone through, some more than once, what we call "the brain stuff." Thanks, Margie Reitz, Chris Moon, Debbie Sellmann, Juli May, Kathy Mullinax, Jan Crossan, Nancy Edge, Katherine Holmes, Trish Manuel, Shelley McDaris, Faith Scheidt, Twila Braun, Dana Burns, Jakki Leatherberry and Kim Martinez for listening and helping me work out the kinks.

I always have to thank my son, Bob Moon, for his help with formatting and publishing.

And there would be no material for study without E. James Wilder, Ph.D., my friend and mentor. Also, thanks go to Chris and Jen Coursey for the THRIVE conferences and to Ed Khouri and Dr. Karl Lehman for all that I have gleaned from their works. Thanks for material that changes our brains and changes our lives.

---

[1]   Barbara   Moon,   *Handbook   to   Joy-Filled   Parenting*, www.lulu.com/barbaramoon 2006

INTRODUCTION

There is not much in life that all of us long for more than loving connections, warm feelings of belonging and unconditional acceptance. We are designed for real relationships with each other and God. We stumble and struggle to find people and places where these yearnings can be met, only to discover quite often that relationships are not only wonderful but very messy. For many, the two most natural responses to the messy spots are either to wallow in them or run away from them. After experiencing the ups and downs of relationships, we can begin to wonder if the search for love, belonging and acceptance is a fleeting hope.

If God designed us for close, intimate relationships, why are they so difficult to find and enjoy? We can find answers by understanding how God designed our brains to function in relationships, receiving healing for hurts from the past, and locking in on the truth that sets us free—all pathways to joy-filled relationships and renewing our minds.

Since 2007 I have been using my parenting book, *Handbook to Joy-Filled Parenting*, in my small group studies, to explore how God designed us for joy-filled relationships. It was clear to me that the principles from four chapters of the parenting book apply to all relationships, not just to parenting, so I began to use those principles to teach the brain science of relationships to my women's groups. I invite you to join me in this study as we look at some practical ways to wade through the difficult, messy places right into the wonderful connections for which we all long.

I learned many of these practical ways to wade through messy places from E. James Wilder, Ph.D., director of Shepherd's House Inc. in Pasadena, CA. Since before 2002, Dr. Wilder has been sharing how God designed the brain to work best in joyful relationships while showing how God's design of the brain fits with Scripture. Through the years, Dr. Wilder and others have written books and developed conferences and materials for both counselors and lay people. The following websites are full of cutting-edge information and quality resources for further study of what Dr. Wilder has named *neurotheology—the mixture of brain science and Scripture.* In *neurotheology*, we discover how the physical design of the brain intersects with Paul's admonition to have renewed minds. I give grateful credit to all at the following websites who have contributed to my information and will be specific when appropriate:

www.lifemodel.org;   www.thrivetoday.org;
www.thrivingrecovery.org;   www.kclehman.com .

Because of the success I've had using the *Handbook to Joy-Filled Parenting* chapters to teach relationships, for this book I have taken the four chapters from that book that contain *The Life Model* and the brain science information, added material that I have gleaned from several sources based on *The Life Model* and THRIVE Conferences, and edited here and there for clarity. The result is a smaller book that can be used in groups or for personal study of how God designed our brains for joyful relationships. I did not remove all references to parenting for two reasons: 1) Looking from a parenting viewpoint we can see the ideal that God has in mind for how our brains should work. 2) I know that parents will consider the material from those four chapters in light of what they did or did not do as parents. That will be the temptation, but I highly encourage everyone to do this study for themselves first.

In the back of the book there are study questions, along with practical exercises for re-training the brain. The exercises are part of the THRIVE conferences given by Chris and Jen Coursey at www.thrivetoday.org and used with permission.

Along with the brain exercises for re-training and/or calming, I encourage all readers to do the practical steps that are suggested within the chapters, whether answering personal questions or making lists. This is a personal study and I will be talking to *you*. The study is not a left-brained, intellectual gathering of knowledge, but rather a right-brained, experiential, practical path to re-training. The study makes us think, makes us see what we did not receive growing up that we were supposed to receive, brings regrets of what we did not know years ago, and requires action that will change our lives. There will be some pain involved, but freedom is just around the corner.

I personally found freedom from this life-changing material. I had a good foundation in Scripture, grace, ministry, counseling and relating, but until I found Dr. Wilder's material, I did not understand where emotional maturity fit in relationships, how joy and the six negative emotions affected the brain and what it meant to "suffer well" and stay relational during intense emotions. I found helpful answers to these dilemmas, and many others, as I understood how traumas affect our relationships, how understanding our brains can help us deal with emotional pain and how emotional healing works when processed through the pathways God designed in the brain.

Not only have I had personal growth and healing from this material, it has greatly changed how I minister to others. The material contained here could be a handbook for counselors and others who minister to hurting people. Truth and healing are both necessary for growth as are both Scripture and intimacy with Jesus. It is not either-or. I pray that all who read and study here will find growth, maturity, healing, freedom and enhanced ministry.

While writing *Handbook to Joy-Filled Parenting*, I was living with my son, Greg, his wife, Chris and their four girls, Tyler, Kayli, Kori and Brenna. (As of this writing, they are now almost 16, 13, 13, and almost 12). Throughout the parenting book, I used pictures of the girls to illustrate various points, as they were the correct ages for the brain development I was discussing. There are a few pictures of my grandsons, Connor & Ryan Patterson and one of another grandson, Aaron. My granddaughter, Erica, is in one picture and not pictured in this book are the other grandchildren, Josh, Elysia, and Jake. (A good grandmother must not leave any unmentioned.) Hopefully the pictures will serve as helpful illustrations.

Barbara Moon October 2012

"And do not be conformed to this world, but be transformed by the renewing of your mind, that you may prove what the will of God is, that which is good and acceptable and perfect." Romans 12:2

NOTES FOR GROUP LEADERS

Joy-Filled Relationships is not only a resource for life-changing information; it is a practical book as well, beneficial to both readers and small group members. Using the material in a group setting will encourage discussion and growth of new relational skills with God and others as members discuss the study questions and do the practical, brain re-training exercises from the Appendix. As the leader, you can use all or part of the questions in the Appendix, but I highly encourage you to do all the exercises.

As you go through the chapters there will be a few places where members will be asked to make lists or answer questions. Chapter One on maturity can be covered in two weeks or stretched to more depending on how much time you want to spend on the five maturity stages. Chapter Three will probably need two weeks as there are five brain levels to learn.

I recommend that you briefly check out each chapter, perhaps by reading the introductions and summaries of each chapter. You can skim the corresponding study questions and exercises in the Appendix in order to have an overview of how the book is set up. After going over the *first six* chapters, it would be possible to skip to other chapters if you want to do so.

I pray that readers or group members will be blessed by the information and changed both by learning to hear God's voice better, and by learning exercises that will re-train their brains.

SECTION I—THE BASICS

CHAPTER ONE: MATURITY

Goal: to act like myself and stay relational regardless of intense emotions

INTRODUCTION

As we begin our study, we are going take a detailed look at maturity—what it is and what it is not, how to evaluate our own and others' maturity and how maturity affects relationships. There will be comprehensive lists from the *Life Model Study Guide,* a guide for the book, *Life Model, Living from the Heart Jesus Gave You,* used with permission. These maturity lists come from years of study at Shepherd's House Ministry. They include five levels or stages of growth that we should ideally progress through over our lifetime. These stages are Infant, Child, Adult, Parent, and Elder.[2]

Before you begin to evaluate your maturity level, let's take a closer look at our goal statement above: ***to act like myself and stay relational regardless of intense emotions***. We will be looking at this goal statement in various ways but for now, let's define it as "acting my age,

---

[2] *The Life Model, Living from the Heart Jesus Gave You*, Shepherd's House, Inc., Van Nuys, CA., 2000; www.lifemodel.org

coping maturely, when something distressing happens." We can also look at it two other ways: "What is like me uniquely?" "What is it like Jesus to do here?"

Here are a few questions that might also help us understand the goal: "What kind of person do you want for your paramedic if you have a heart attack?" "Who do you want with you if your child has an accident or gets very sick?" "How do you act if your car gets scratched?" The different reactions people have to distress can be a sign of their maturity. We all want a paramedic who will remain calm and knowledgeable when someone has a heart attack. If we've lost our child at the state fair, we want a calm and proficient policeman or friend to help. We want these helpers to act like themselves and be able to communicate with us during the distress. We would be quite unhappy if they were indulging in an addiction or fell apart and could not function at the time we needed help. In the same way, maturity can help us stay calm when daily stressors bombard us as we live in our families, our work places and communities. Maturity will keep us from attacking the person who scratched our new car—although we might have strong *feelings* about something we *wish* we could do about the scratched car.

Maturity is a central truth we all need to understand. In today's world and even in the Church, maturity is seldom discussed. All sorts of messages shouting "how-to" and "you should" bombard us, but we do not hear enough messages shouting, "Grow up!" I am personally on a mission to bring up the concept of "maturity" whenever I can. As I walk through life and interact with others about problems that they or their friends are having, when possible, I point out that maturity may be the issue. What I mean by maturity is not spiritual maturity, but emotional maturity, the kind of maturity that helps us act like the age we are supposed to be. A person can have an adult body, know tons of Scripture, be a leader at work and at church and still be at Infant or Child maturity emotionally. Maturity is not necessarily about chronological age.

We all know adults (chronologically) who whine, pout, blow up or attack when they don't get their way. The body may grow to adulthood while the person emotionally stays in a younger stage. To be at the maturity level that matches our chronological age, we must complete each task shown on the lists below. As we mature through the stages with all of their needs and tasks, those needs and tasks must carry forward to the next stage. We cannot skip a stage.

Now let's look at some questions that prepare you to evaluate your own maturity level as you look at the stages from the *Life Model*. Take a few minutes to answer them here or on a sheet of paper.

Do I know what satisfies the way God defines satisfaction?

Do I know how to do hard things or do I procrastinate?

Can I bring two or more people back to joy (reconnect after conflict) at the same time?

Do I know the characteristics of my own heart?

Am I able to regulate my own emotions?

Do I know how to ask for what I need?

Do I know how to give without expecting anything in return?

Do I protect others from myself so as not to hurt them?

What have I used to measure maturity?

As you look through the five maturity stages, keep your answers nearby and consider the answers you gave to these questions. You will see what stage these questions came from.

When we look at the maturity stages, we will see the essential needs and tasks for maturity, used by permission, from *The Life Model Guide*.[3] Each stage builds on the previous stage; therefore, each stage includes the needs, what we should receive from others, and tasks, what we learn to do ourselves, of the previous stage. No stage can be skipped. The "ideal age" is the earliest age at which new tasks can be attempted. The end of that stage expects some degree of mastery. In no way does our maturity determine our value, but it does determine the level of responsibility we can handle.

Because the list of maturity stages is copyrighted, the levels will be listed as they are written, but underneath each need or task you will see questions that can help you better understand the need or task. I thought it might help to first give you some definitions for the terms that are included in the list of needs and tasks. They will be in the order that they appear in the list of stages.

---

[3] *The Life Model Study Guide*, Shepherd's House Inc., Pasadena, CA, 2002

MATURITY: Completeness and wholeness at a given level.

EARNED MATURITY: The level of maturity at which one has completed the given needs and tasks, regardless of chronological age.

JOY: Someone is glad to be with me, I am the sparkle in someone's eye.

JOY BONDS: An attachment or bond with another person that is based on being glad to be together versus being based on fear.

THE EYES OF HEAVEN: The way God looks at our world and us.

RECEIVE & GIVE LIFE: Actions/attitudes that communicate love and caring and that build up another.

SYNCHRONIZE: To match energy and be on the 'same page' with another.

ORGANIZE SELF INTO A PERSON: Form one's unique personality

RETURN TO JOY: To be glad to be together in distress and/or reconnect with someone who hurt me.

REST: Calm oneself, experience peace.

WEANING: Leave mother's world and go out into the community.

NUCLEUS ACCUMBENS: An area of the brain that is commonly called the "pleasure center." It screams, "I must have _____ or I will die!"

RITE OF PASSAGE: An event or time when a young person is honored for becoming an adult.

INCLUSION IN SAME-SEX COMMUNITY: Men spend time with boys and women spend time with girls, helping pave the way into adulthood.

USING POWER FAIRLY: Not abusing those under us who have less power because of their age or position; allowing age appropriate choices without extreme penalties.

SHARE LIFE IN PARTNERSHIP: Learning to compromise for the good of all concerned; preparation for marriage, business, and/or living in a community.

PROCLAIM PERSONAL AND GROUP IDENTITY: Know where one fits in a group and be able to stand for that group if attacked.

BRING SELF & OTHERS BACK TO JOY: The ability to help oneself, and others, to reconnect after conflict so that all are satisfied.

PEER REVIEW: Finding and receiving accountability from peers.

GIVE WITHOUT RECEIVING IN RETURN: When one does not expect a reward of any kind for all that he or she has done for another.

GIVING LIFE TO THOSE WITHOUT FAMILY: Helping and showing hospitality, "adopting" those who for various reasons have no family.

ACT LIKE ONESELF DURING DIFFICULTY: To exhibit mature actions and attitudes without falling apart during distress.

THE STAGES

E. James Wilder, Ph.D., Questions by Barbara Moon

All rights reserved

THE INFANT STAGE   Ideal Age: Birth to Age 4

Infant Needs

1. Joy Bonds with both parents that are strong, loving, caring, secure

   (Did I have a loving caring secure bond with each parent? What if my bonds were fear based? If so, do I **now** have a loving caring bond with a woman? Do I have one with a man?)

2. Important needs are met without asking

   (Were my needs met in these first 3-4 years without me asking? One has to receive before giving. The adults met my needs instead of me being the "parent." If it was reversed, how have I dealt with that?)

3. Quiet together time

   (Do I know how to quiet myself? Do I regularly have quiet together with another person? With God? (This is quietness inside, not just sitting still.))

4. Help regulating distressing emotions

   (How am I doing with the Big Six emotions? (Anger, Sad, Fear, Disgust, Hopeless, Shame))

12   © 2012 Barbara Moon

5.   Be seen through the "eyes of Heaven"

(Do I know I am accepted and loved outside of my behavior? Do I accept myself based on Heaven's eyes? Do I have at least one person who sees me this way?)

6.   Receive and give life

(Can I receive without guilt or shame? Do I think I have to "give all the time?" Can I do good things for myself without feeling guilty?)

7.   Have others synchronize with him/her first

(Can I allow another to help me, comfort me and synchronize with me without feeling guilt or shame? *Comforting a crying baby teaches hope.*)

Infant Tasks

1.   Receive with joy

(Can I receive with joy without feeling guilty or refusing the gesture? Do I try to keep others from serving me, helping me? Am I able to just say "thank you?")

2.   Learn to synchronize with others

(Am I learning to synchronize (be in tune with) with others of all ages?)

3.   Organize self into a person through imitation

(Babies learn who they are by imitation, not instructions. Whoever pays attention to them is the one(s) they model after in these years. The attention can be positive or negative. They go by the face and what they see there to determine their worth and identity. Their cries are asking for help to feel better.)

(Do I know who I am as a person? What is like me? Whom did I imitate growing up? What was my principle caretaker like? Have I had or do I have someone in my life now to help me form an identity or improve it?)

4.   Learn to regulate emotion

(Baby learns to regulate by being allowed to rest before she is overwhelmed. Mother synchronizes and knows when to allow rest during the joy building.)

5.   Learn to return to joy from every emotion

(Can I be myself when upset in all the emotions? Which ones am I good at, which am I lacking? How do I handle disappointment and humiliation?)

6.   Learn to be the same person over time

(Am I the same person when upset as when I am in joy? Would others say I am moody and different when angry or upset? Do I have someone to help me learn the missing skills?)

7.   Learn self-care skills

(Am I able to take care of myself? At this stage, just myself is enough. As an adult that might mean saying "no" to things or asking for help when needed.)

8.   Learn to rest

(Can I rest and not be hyper or intense all the time? This means inside rest as well as outside. Am I willing to learn this and do I have someone to help me with it?)

THE CHILD STAGE   Ideal Age: Ages 4-13

I have taken some of my comments here from *Living With Men,* by Dr. James Wilder.[4] At this age, the child will begin to branch out more into "daddy's world." She will begin to venture further from mom than before, growing into some independence, knowing mom is there for reassurance and help. Mom will no longer guess at the needs, the child will begin to ask and receive. If the child has had a close bond, he or she will know that someone will comfort them when bad things happen. He doesn't have to fear adversity and pain. She knows there is a path back to joy. He does not have to control others to get needs met. She knows how to use her words.

Child Needs

1. Weaning

    (Weaning is the end of infancy and only done well by well-trained four-year old brains. If the child was raised on fear, weaning will not go well. He or she will not know their needs and feelings.)

    (Have I healthily separated from my mother? Do I expect people to read my mind? Can I take care of myself? What kind of relationship did I have with my father? Did he respond positively to my requests for needs? Did he show me how to increasingly take care of myself and broaden my world? Did I learn to go out on "adventures" and return home to rest?)

---

[4] E. James Wilder, Ph.D., *The Complete Guide to Living with Men,* Shepherd's House, Inc. Pasadena, CA 2004

2. Help to do what he does not feel like doing

(Can I do things I do not feel like doing? Do I understand that others do not *only* do what they feel like doing? This skill learned around the age of five prepares us to be able to do hard things.)

3. Help sorting feelings, imaginations and reality

(Can I separate feelings, imaginations and reality? Do I understand how the "real world" operates? Do I know how to judge if my feelings are real or not? Do I believe everything I feel? Do I have someone in my life that I can trust to tell me the truth and help me change my understanding when I have a misconception?)

4. Feedback on guesses, attempts and failures

(Have I been allowed to learn through my mistakes without being overly punished or rejected? Am I confident to take appropriate risks or am I overly performance based?)

5. Be taught the family history

(Do I know how my family came to be? This comes around the age of twelve. Was I taught how my actions would affect history? Did I hear stories of my family history? Was I taught how to avoid continuing the negative parts of my family history?)

6. Be taught the history of God's family

(Do I know the story of God's family? Was I taught how to truly live by knowing the stories and people of the One who gives life and knows how to do it? If not, am I learning that now?)

7. Be taught the "big picture" of life

    (Do I understand the big picture of life? Do I understand consequences of my behavior can affect generations? Did I learn that I am not entitled to things without working? Was I prepared to become an adult by having a map that showed the path to maturity?

Child Tasks

1. Take care of self (one is enough right now)

    (Do I know how to take care of myself by saying, "No," when necessary? Did I receive love that I did not have to earn? Can I look back and notice any of the identity changes I have gone through? Did I have to take care of someone else when too young?)

2. Learn to ask for what he/she needs

    (Do I know how to ask for what I need? Do I not expect others to read my mind and guess what I need? Can I ask without feeling guilty? (Unmet needs produce anger.))

3. Learn self-expression

    (Am I able to enjoy myself without feeling guilty or inhibited? Can I express myself and not have to have someone else talk for me?)

4. Develop personal resources and talents

    (Am I growing at what I am good at? Do I know my talents and spiritual gifts?)

5. Learn to make himself/herself understandable to others

    (If someone misunderstands me, do I try in a calm way to help him or her understand me?)

6. Learn to do hard things

    (Do I know how to do hard things? This is more than just getting up to go to work. It is also emotionally hard things—like facing pain and not avoiding it. I can actually choose to do hard things even if they hurt.)

7. Learn what satisfies

    (Do I know what satisfies? Satisfaction has a 24-hour shelf life, so it needs to be renewed each day. Some things that satisfy are sharing joy, doing hard things and getting through them, receiving and giving life, food, love, efforts. I know I am entitled to have my needs met. I receive joyfully, but also give cheerfully so as not to be only a consumer. I was not expected to sacrificially give before I was mature enough. (Ecclesiastes 8:15))

8. Tame the *nucleus accumbens*--our cravings

    (Have I tamed my cravings? (Genesis 25: 27-32) or I am working on that and have someone to help me and keep me accountable? If I have addictions, am I admitting it and getting help?)

9. See self through the "eyes of Heaven"

    (Do I see myself through Heaven's eyes because someone else has seen or is seeing me that way? Am I at least learning how God looks at me?)

THE ADULT STAGE   Ideal Age: Age 13-first child

Adult Needs

1.   A rite of passage

(Do I remember any kind of "rite of passage" as I became a teen? What might we as a family like to do for our children as they become this age? Was I prepared well for becoming an adult?)

2.   Time to bond with peers and form a group identity

(How did I progress through my teen years? Was I allowed to form a group identity? Did I choose a group that was a good or a bad influence? Did my community help me with a group identity?)

3.   Inclusion by the same-sex community

(Did I have community with other men or women growing up? Do I have community with other men or women now? Do I feel included?)

4.   Observing the same sex using their power fairly

(Can I use my power fairly? Do I know how to negotiate and compromise? Have I seen this modeled by other men or women?)

5.   Being given important tasks by his/her community

(Was I given important tasks growing up? Do I feel I have an important place in my community now? (The Mormons do this with their young men who are required to serve 2 years). What is the main ingredient needed when we give young people an important task? We have to TRUST them. What if they fail? Jesus trusted the untrustworthy without condemning their failures.)

6. Guidance for the personal imprint they will make on history

(Do I realize that because I am alive, life will not be the same for other people? Was I told how my behavior could affect history? Do I understand that now? *(The movie, It's a Wonderful Life is an example of this))*

7. Opportunities to share life in partnership

(Have I had opportunities to share life in partnership? Have I practiced being in partnership with peers and older adults?)

Adult Tasks

1. Take care of two or more at the same time

(Am I able to take emotional and physical care of two or more at the same time? Can I negotiate and compromise so that all are satisfied? Do I understand the real meaning of fairness? (A good analogy--A real estate agent's main job is to discover what everyone needs and bring all to satisfaction in the negotiations.))

2. Discover the main characteristics of his/her heart

(Do I know the main characteristics of my heart? Do I know what hurts me and how that pain shows me the characteristics of my heart? Have I had or do I have someone who tells me the truth about my heart, encouraging me and supporting me as I live with a heart like mine and the pain it can bring? Do I know the spiritual disciplines that help me take care of my heart? **(See Dyad Discussion 2 for Chapter One in the Appendix.)**

3. Proclaim and defend personal and community(group)identity

(Can I tell others who I am and who my community is? Cults and gangs do this. Christianity calls it evangelism-- telling the Good News.)

4.   Bring self and others back to joy simultaneously

(Can I bring myself and others back to joy (reconnect) at the same time. Do I maintain who I am and act like myself when distress and conflict come? Adults realize, "We can do this together." Can I be glad to be with those in the shadows by being with them where they are? Are others glad to be with the "real me" or someone I want them to think I am? Do I have any relationships that are estranged and need repair? (This does not include unsafe relationships))

5.   Develop a personal style that reflects his/her heart

(Is there any part of myself I am rejecting? Have I embraced all of my uniqueness?)

6.   Learn to protect others from himself/herself

(Do I protect others from myself by removing myself when not able to stay calm and act like myself? Do I manipulate to get my own way? Am I able to interact without overwhelming another? Do I notice when someone says, "ouch!" Do I ask forgiveness when I hurt others? *(It is very important to recognize that something hurts. Many have avoided or repressed pain or been taught that it is not okay to know/admit that something hurts—for reasons such as, others may not care, no comfort, no support, codependency, etc. We have to say it hurts when it hurts.))*

7.   Learn to diversify and blend roles

(Can I function healthily and with balance in various roles that I am called to do?)

8.   Life-giving sexuality

(Do I know what it means to have life-giving sexuality? Have I had healing and/or redemption of any non life-giving sexuality from my past? Do I understand why God has instructions about this area of life?)

9. Mutual satisfaction in a relationship

    (Do I know how to find a compromise that will satisfy both people in a relationship? Do I have to always win? Do I know how to share and use my power wisely? *(Some ways to share power with children are things such as allowing them to have a say so about their rooms, helping them achieve goals, not being overly strict, allowing failures and mistakes, allowing age appropriate decisions.))*

10. Partnership

    (Partnership in marriage (and other relationships) is like buddy breathing on a deep-sea dive. It is like working out on many different machines at the gym in order to develop different muscles. (p. 116 *Living With Men*))

THE PARENT STAGE — Ideal age: From first child until the youngest child becomes an adult at 13

Parent Needs

1. To give life

    (Do I know what it means to "give life?" What is the opposite of giving life? Does one have to have a biological child to be a "life giver," and a "parent?")
    (Have I looked at the kind of bond I had with my parents and how that can affect my parenting? Do I know my limitations as a parent? Bonds will be different with each child and bonds can change.)

2. An encouraging partner

(Do I have an encouraging partner? If single, what does that mean? With my spouse, do I know that intimacy is not diminished when shared?)

3. Guidance from elders

(Am I getting guidance from Elders? I need encouragement as I am stretched.}

4. Peer review from other fathers and mothers

(Am I in a community with other fathers and mothers? Do I have someone to talk to about parenting? Am I open to input from other parents? Am I working to keep my marriage going well during the busyness of parenting? Will I have someone to help me with all the stages of parenting?)

5. A secure and orderly environment

(Do I live in a secure and orderly environment or am I surrounded by chaos? What needs to change for my environment to be more secure? More orderly?)

Parent Tasks

1. Giving without needing to receive in return

(Can I, or am I learning to give without receiving anything in return? This task is one of the most important tasks of the parent stage. It begins the day the first child is born and never ends. It will make or break you and highly determine what kind of person you will be and what kind of children you will rear. It is very difficult to learn if one has not gone through most of the parts of the previous stages. This stage costs you your life (time, energy, resources). The cost of something shows its value, how much it is loved. Can I rejoice in the call to unselfishness?))

2.   Building a home

(Am I building a home that reflects God's ways and His life? Am I taking advantage of opportunities to learn and grow in order to make a better home?)

3.   Protecting his/her family

(Do I know what it means to protect my family? Do I protect them from myself when necessary by disengaging but not putting up a wall? (Am I too overprotective? Am I too dismissive?)

4.   Serving his/her family

(Am I serving my family? Do I expect a good balance for sharing household chores? Do I model a Biblical view of servant hood? This does not mean I do "everything."

Enjoying his/her family

(Do I know how to enjoy my family? Am I interested in my family members as individuals? Do I know how to have fun without being hurtful? Do I know how to include everyone? Look at Zephaniah 3:17, an example of a great parent.)

5.   Helping his/her children reach maturity

(Am I working on my own maturity and learning how to help my children reach their full potential? Do I look at my children as unique individuals and accept them as God has made them? Do I know where to go for help when needed? Do I take care of myself so I will be able to take care of others?)

(As one grows through the parenting of each child, each child and each stage the child goes through brings out different aspects of the parent's heart. Each brings out areas that need healing and growth. We will review and retrace ourselves with each child. In order to grow, I must face my pain. If I don't, the bond will break and the child will be crippled. This is all training for the Elder Stage, which is highly unselfish.)

6. Synchronizing with the developing needs of: children, spouse, family, work and church

    (Am I able to synchronize with all the people and the areas of life, being able to do more than one thing at a time when necessary? Do I have a working system for keeping track of all the family schedules? Do I remember the emotional needs that my family has and spend the necessary time it takes to help them? Am I able to satisfy more than one person at a time? Am I being careful not to do "Elder work" before my family is ready? Do I keep a balance of outside activities that might take too much time from my family?)

THE ELDER STAGE   Ideal age: Youngest child is an adult (age 13)

From *Living With Men,* by E. James Wilder—Elder is the longest developmental stage and the most slow-growing. It will last the longest. The Elder harmonizes many aspects of the community. A person who lived and motivated others through fear will not reach Elder maturity. They will be rigid, controlling and shriveled in their thinking. True

Elders are known by how they can grasp complexity and respond with simple directness. Elders are at a place where their control is decreasing but their investment in people is increasing. Elders will make mistakes as they learn and they need community support during that time.

Elder Needs

1. A community to call his/her own

2. Recognition by his/her community

    (Do I have a community to which I belong and where I am recognized as an elder?)

3. A proper place in the community structure

    (Am I building trust through warmth, authenticity and transparency? Am I good at telling stories?)

4. Have others trust them

    (Do others trust me because I have earned and proven my trustworthiness?)

5. Be valued and protected by their community

    (Does my community value me for who I am? Am I teaching my community how to recover from mistakes, both my own and others'? Do I stay involved when things get tough? Does the community protect me when that is necessary?)

Elder Tasks

1. Hospitality

    (Am I known as a welcoming person, warm and approachable? Am I easy to talk to? Am I willing to use my resources to help those without?)

2.   Giving life to those without families

(Am I involved where possible in helping those who need a Spiritual family? One of the first aspects of the Elder stage is having a new son or daughter-in-law. This is part of welcoming new people into the family—both natural and spiritual. Then Elders bond with children they did not produce (grandchildren). As the bonds are extended, this forms the community. Elders become "parents" to those without a good family. They "adopt" adults to help them become parents, just as adults "adopt" children to help them become adults.)

3.   Parent and mature his/her community

(Can others look to me to do safe, parent-like things in my community such as love everyone, build joy, kiss all the babies, give resources to bad risks, hug and snuggle and give back rubs (p. 226 *Living With Men*)? Do I know how to build trust in a safe environment? I have to be known as a very safe person.)

4.   Build and maintain a community identity

(Am I helping my community build and maintain its identity? Do I help when changes come along that might threaten that identity?)

5.   Act like him/herself in the midst of difficulty

(Am I able to remain myself during distress and quiet myself and others? Do I bring stability and lessen anxiety? Can I bring myself and others back to joy? If I am in emotional pain myself, can I suffer well and remember what is important?)

6.   Enjoy what God puts in each person in the community
       (Seeing each of them through "eyes of Heaven")

       (Am I able to enjoy the value in all kinds of people and build
       joy as much as possible?)

7.   Building the trust of others through the elder's own
       transparency and spontaneity

       (Am I transparent, vulnerable, open and spontaneous? Do I
       understand the importance of not keeping secrets? Do I
       understand that these qualities are how trust is built and that
       others do not trust someone who is hiding things, even their
       responses? Can I be joyfully spontaneous, giving and fun?
       [In the brain, trust is built the same place that we learn to
       recognize and interpret faces. Trust is built over time, face to
       face, with honest authentic people who share our feelings. (p.
       237 *Living With Men*))

READ JOB 29:12-17

# # # #

I hope that you have now gone prayerfully through the stages,
comparing them to the list of questions you answered, and have at least
one or two areas that God has shown you that you could use help.
Write one or two here:

_____

_____

_____

© 2012 Barbara Moon

If by chance you got overwhelmed by the list and found so many you felt hopeless, get in touch with a friend or other helping person and begin the process to work through your needs. Take no shame or condemnation for whatever level you may have. Your background greatly determines your maturity level and God loves to heal us and grow us. He desires to bring us to "earned maturity" that corresponds to our chronological age.

Earned maturity means that we have completed the needs and tasks for a certain stage of maturity. Chronological age does not necessarily correspond to earned maturity. When working through issues where earning maturity is taking place later than the ideal age, it takes perseverance and willingness to deal with pain from the past. It might involve counseling to discover where we got stuck in the process of growing up. We might have to explore the traumas that happened to us and arrested our emotional growth. God is ready and willing to heal us. We will find ways to receive His healing from painful traumas in later chapters in this book.

The *Life Model* describes two types of traumas—Type A traumas wounded us when there was an "**A**bsence of good things," when we did not receive the things in life that we were supposed to get. Type B traumas wounded us when "**B**ad things happened." Hard work, humility, joy and willingness to admit needs are prerequisites to going back and completing needed tasks, while recovering from traumas. Traumas and neglect keep us from completing the maturity tasks and our emotional growth becomes stuck. In order to get unstuck we need to have relationships based on love bonds and to identify the needs and wounds from Type A and Type B traumas.

Let's look at some examples that describe maturity or "completeness and wholeness at a given level." For example, if one is old enough to have a car—there is a level at which that person should be complete and whole—the adult level. The law says we must have reached a certain chronological age. Emotionally to be at the adult level, we must have grown through all the previous stages on the list and carried them forward. Even though one is old enough to have a car, it's possible that one is not mature enough. So let's take one of my favorite tasks for evaluating the emotional maturity of the adult stage, "protecting others from him or herself," and apply it to a person's reaction to a scratched car.

In a distressing, highly emotional moment such as a scratched car, we can quickly see if a person is protecting others from him or herself. Let's say the car gets scratched and anger rises. If I verbally attack someone, is that an example of protecting that person from myself? Not at all. If I blow up, am I acting like myself and staying relational? Not really. At this moment I am not "giving life." I am giving "death." This kind of situation and knowing how to assess maturity can act as a red flag to help me see where I need to grow and mature according to the unmet need or unmet task in that level.

Maybe a scratched car does not set you off. But an argument with your spouse does. Are you able to come to "mutual satisfaction in a relationship" or do you *have* to win and get your way? Do you see the conflict as my way/your way or a place to come to compromise where all are satisfied? An adult knows how to compromise for mutual satisfaction.

As a parent do you remind yourself that you are "giving without needing to receive in return?" When you get up for the third time in the middle of the night are you able to act like yourself? The same way you ask yourself questions, you can, as a parent looking at the stage that corresponds to your child's age, ask yourself questions from the lists to determine if he or she is on level. For example: Is my three to four year old doing fairly well at regulating his emotions? Is she beginning to take care of herself at her level? Is my six year old able to ask for what he needs and make himself understandable to others? Does my teenager understand how his actions will make an imprint on history?

Dr. Wilder has a great illustration to help assess whether a teenager is a "child" or an "adult." He points out that if a young person understands his affect on history, he will not be as prone to behave "unseemly" in the back seat of a car. Pre-marital sex and pregnancies cause shock waves through more than one generation. A man realizes the consequences of sex outside of marriage and a boy does not. When young people understand that their actions can have ramifications for generations, they will be less likely to make choices that might bring disaster on their family both now and in the future. A young person in the adult stage will better understand that a sexual relationship is for bringing "life" to others, not "death."

These kinds of questions make it easier to assess where we are. And just as our maturity level could be lower than our chronological age, we can also try to do tasks in a higher stage before we are ready. Parents of young families must be careful not to be doing Elder stage work to an extent that the young family suffers. It's possible to become so involved in helping our churches and our communities that we are not at home to help our own families. We would not expect our two year old to babysit her new brother, nor do we want our fifteen year old to become a parent.

Working on our own maturity is absolutely vital in light of family, marriage and parenting, as is monitoring the growth of our children. Since more is caught than taught and we cannot pass on to our children that which we don't have ourselves, how can we ignore this issue of maturity? The list of stages can help us see more easily what we need to work on. Let your community help you mature so that your children and your family will benefit. Let God show you where you are lacking and have the courage to admit it and get help.

Where you may be lacking in maturity does not in any way diminish your value. As we work through maturity issues, it is extremely important to remember that maturity is not about value nor is it a place to take shame. Instead of determining value by maturity or immaturity, we can look at a person's level of maturity the way Dr. Wilder says it in *Living With Men*, "I am just not ready for that yet." When we look at infants, we know that they are valuable even though they can *do* nothing that seems valuable. Babies are right where they are supposed to be while growing through the needs and tasks pertaining to their first four years of life. Babies can smile and bring joy to us, but they are not ready for kindergarten. Six year olds are not ready to date and fourteen year olds are not ready for marriage. We can only mature as we journey through each need and task, even if that means going back and picking up where we might be stuck. Just because a person is not ready for something does not diminish his or her value. So as an adult, don't get down on yourself, or anyone else, if you need to grow in an area. Keep in mind that it is all right to say, "I am not ready for that yet, but I am working, or want to work, on getting there."

How do we as adults work on growing through that level where we may be stuck? What is God's part and what is our part? From the Scripture, Dr. Wilder has separated these responsibilities quite well, although they overlap with each other as to cooperation. He says that salvation, deliverance, healing and redemption are God's responsibility. Maturing is a human's responsibility; it is not a spiritual gift (James 1:4). Maturing was not automatic during our childhood years and it won't be automatic now. Working on the unmet needs and unmet tasks requires courage and co-operation with God's guidance and leading, as we do our part with support from loving relationships. We do the hard work that it takes to grow up—to ask for help, to talk about and feel our unresolved pain, to get accountability from others who are willing to speak truth to us.

As you think about this short list of hard things that make growing up difficult, it is easy to see that maturing is a job for the community. *Maturing is not the job for a spouse*, though spouses will be supportive and encouraging. It will take authentic relationships with people who are trustworthy to tell us where the lacks are and to support us while we go back through a missed task, while we look at the Absence of good things that were supposed to happen (Type A traumas) and any Bad things that happened (Type B traumas). Small groups at church, loving family and close friends are good places for finding the community support we need. Keep in mind that maturing can be a *very long and slow process* and give yourself and others plenty of grace to move along.

SUMMARY

Maturity is a misunderstood and seldom-discussed topic. Growing up, many of us have missed the needs and tasks for natural progression through the maturity stages. The lacks from Type-A traumas and the bad things that happened to us keep us stuck in stages below our chronological age. In order to mature, we need a loving community with authentic relationships. It is important to get healing from any traumas that might have arrested our growth. We need a church and a small group that can encourage us, and we might need a good counselor. How we grow personally and as a parent greatly affects our children's growth. We need to be the kind of person we want our children to become. As we mature and work on what we missed, we remember that we are very valuable no matter the level of maturity we have earned.

CHAPTER TWO: INTRODUCING THE TECHNICAL WHYS

Goal: to begin understanding terms and the importance of the brain science research

INTRODUCTION

In the next chapter we will look briefly at the new brain research, but before we go there, let's take a look at some definitions and a short overview. It is my goal to walk you through the technical whys one piece at a time. I have left much of the information about parenting in this section as it will help us understand why the information is important. In Chapters Three and Four we will look at the importance of synchronization, the importance of building joy and quiet, and returning to joy. These chapters are vital for you to understand the importance of this brain science research and how God's ideal for brain development affects, not only the newborn's emotional and relational development through the first two years, but all relationships. Living in joy as God designed the brain affects all relationships throughout life.

In order to make the next chapters easier to understand, below you will find definitions for some of the new terms that will appear in those chapters. The definitions are in alphabetical order and a few are repetitive. Referring to these definitions may help you as you go through the chapters, looking at material that is probably new to most of us. I will speak more within the chapters about each topic.

ACTING LIKE MYSELF: Behaving in a manner that fits my maturity level, my unique personhood and the characteristics of my heart.

ATTACHMENT: Another word for bonding, connecting or belonging with another person. Sharing a state of mind.

BUILDING JOY: The interaction with another person that results in true emotional joy between the two (or more). This interaction happens non- verbally through joy smiles, eyes that light up, voice tone and proper touch. It means we are glad to be together.

DESYNCHRONIZATION: Not tuning in to what another person is feeling when interacting with them, causing disharmony both emotionally and within the brain.

FLESH (*SARK*): The condition of believing false ideas (lies) about oneself that do not coincide with what God says. Leaning on my own understanding. (Proverbs 3:5-6)

HEART: The human spirit, the essence of a person, where Jesus lives and guides when one is a Christian

JOY BUCKET: A part of our emotional brain, our emotional make-up that, when filled with joy enables us to thrive, relate well and endure hardships, disappointments and trials.

JOY CAMP: The state of being where God designed us to live.

JOY: Someone is glad to be with me and I am the sparkle in someone's eyes. (It takes at least two)

MINDSIGHT: A function of the brain that enables us to focus on ("see") another person's mind and know what they and we are feeling, perceiving, believing, intending. (Siegel)

MOTHER CORE: The part of the brain that enables us to match energy (synchronize) with another person. It is the place where true joy smiles originate, the place that enables us to dance, to have empathy and know there is another mind behind the face we are interacting with.

QUIET TOGETHER: During joy building, the more mature person synchronizes with the other's need to rest and backs off the intensity, allows the other to rest, but does not leave.

RETURN TO JOY: Reconnecting with someone who distressed me. Being glad to be with someone during distressful emotions and helping him or her stay stable or become stable until the distress passes.

STAYING RELATIONAL: Being able to interact in a stable and mature way with others, in spite of distressing emotions in or around us.

SUFFERING WELL: Having enough joy strength to prevent us from "falling apart" when distress comes, and to enable us to stay relational and act like who we are during that time of distress.

SYNCHRONIZATION: The state of being on the same wavelength with another person and sharing energy levels. Synchronizing takes place both emotionally with self and others, as well as physically in the brain.

THE EMOTIONAL CONTROL CENTER: The places in the emotional brain that need to be synchronized in order to function well and thrive.

THRIVING: Developing healthily, having a stable and fully developed life, reaching one's potential.

As we begin to look at the technical side of our study, it may help to compare the "brain stuff" to a computer. We all have goals for our lives and our goals can be compared to the software in a computer. Those "software" goals, such as character qualities, authentic relationships and life skills are like computer software programs that we need instilled in our hearts that will empower us to do and be all that God wants us to be.

But computers need hardware before they can run the software. The hardware is a level below the software that enables the computer to run the software efficiently. This hardware below those goals we set for ourselves is the brain. So in the next few chapters we will take a look at what makes that software run most efficiently. We will evaluate how our hardware is wired up and what might be missing from the way the Designer designed it. To see how the Designer designed the brain, we will look at what is supposed to happen to a child between birth and two years.

Another way to look at how the brain should be wired and what we have received—or missed—is a question from our last chapter where we asked what type of person we all want to have around us in a crisis.

What causes one person to be able to function "like a hero" in a crisis while others around them are falling apart? I believe that part of the answer to both of these questions is the same. Much of the hardware and the capacity to function in a crisis are wired inside of a child during the first two years of his or her life.

During the first two years of a baby's life, critical windows of development open and shut in the brain. In those two years parents can build neurological pathways that will affect the way their child lives and relates as an adult. Why is this so important? What happens in a child's brain through interaction with caregivers affects how he or she will learn to rightly handle the situations and events in their lives that involve pain and distress. How they are wired will determine how they manage what is hard for them to do. If children don't receive what they need most during this period of their lives, it is likely that they will not develop as well as they could. They can learn unhealthy ways of relating that may block them from progressing through the stages of maturity in a natural way. Depending on the input from parents, the interaction with their infant and young child can even strengthen or weaken the child's immune system and how it is going to operate the rest of his life. These first two to three years are crucial as the most ideal time to take advantage of knowing this "brain stuff."

Although we can use the analogy of a computer to look at how our brains work, humans are much more complex and varied than any machine. I'm in no way meaning to diminish other aspects of a person's upbringing or negate that the way God has made each of us is unique and individual. I simply want to get this information out so that we can do as much prevention, and repair, as possible and do our best to break any cycles that keep future babies from getting what they need. We will be looking at how important the primary caregiver is in the process of helping a baby thrive. It will give you insight as to your own needs.

In the next three chapters, we will look at what it takes to build a secure bond, gain the ability to handle distress, and strengthen the capacity to relate to others in healthy ways. We will look at how important it is for all of us to build our capacity to experience joy, because we will only be able to deal with the painful situations in our lives if we have enough joy in our hearts to make it through difficult times.

Although we as readers are past the infant stage, don't worry. There are steps we can take to help retrain our brains (Exercises in the Appendix) and become all God has in mind for us. So read on and find that joy will always be a contributing factor to anyone's life.

As you read on you will see in Chapter Three, what we already know and have in our own brain was passed down to us from our mother or principle caretaker. Mothers actually download part of their brain into their babies' brains, passing down to their children what they had passed down—unless someone helps them learn new ways of relating.

As I learned more about these new ways of relating, the definitions we just looked at, along with some insight into their meanings, gave me answers to some of my relationship questions. In a nutshell, I learned what happens when we interact face to face with each other. I learned the reason why I always hated seeing someone tickle a child until they cried. I learned how important it is to build joy and have quietness with each other. I found out why it does little good to try to convince someone to change their mind about an issue. I learned why words and lectures are not helpful at certain times. I learned why comfort was such an important gift to another. And much of what I learned was a better way to say things that I already knew intuitively. All these insights were valuable and I trust will be helpful to you as well.

SUMMARY

Although the brain science information may sound a little technical, it is life-changing. Knowing how God designed our brains helps us relate better, helps us see what we were supposed to receive growing up and helps us know how to remedy the places we are lacking. I encourage you to learn the new terms as you go through the rest of the book to learn how the "brain stuff" fits with joy-filled relating.

CHAPTER THREE: THE NEW BRAIN STUDIES

Goal: to understand thriving, synchronization and the Emotional Control Center

INTRODUCTION

Now we are almost ready to look at an overview of the brain science research. Keep in mind that this research has to do with the *emotional* aspects of the brain, the Right Hemisphere, not the Left, intellectual side. The right side of the brain is all about relationships. Thanks again to Dr. Wilder for getting it into everyday language. I have his permission to use some of his material from a conference he does on thriving. My interpretations and suggestions will be intermingled. Dr. Wilder has skillfully combined the *Life Model* principles, (based on Scripture) and the brain research to give us a good picture of what it takes to thrive, to fully develop. He correlates the ingredients needed for thriving, or lack of it, to a specific part of the brain. For this book, I feel that most people won't care about the particular brain part, its name (though I will name them) or location, but can be satisfied knowing what it does and why it is important. That is my objective in sharing it at all. If we allow it to, knowing its importance will change the way we relate. So hang in there with me through the definitions and other technical stuff while you look at the whats and whys and hows.

But before we look at the chart that I have modified from Dr. Wilder's conference on thriving, let me ask you some questions as I did in the chapter on maturity. Hopefully wanting answers to these questions will tickle your curiosity about the brain science.

Do you know what it takes for us as humans to develop healthily?

What happens to a person's ability to cope when frightened?

What kind of bond did you have with your parents, especially Mother?

Are you a joy-filled person?

How do you feel when someone is not on the same wavelength you are?

What do you do with emotional pain (like missing someone or hurt feelings)-feel it or medicate it?

Do you know how to calm yourself and others?

Are you open to receive love and connection, or closed and avoidant?

If some of these questions were difficult for you and you're feeling uneasy about what you might need to work on in your life, I would encourage you to look around in your church, your family or your community and find a person who seems to possess some of the qualities you want. Observe how they interact with others. Ask them to help you. They can "download" some of their brain to yours. And stick with me here. You will find good information, practical exercises, and clues to help you with some of the answers to the questions above. Now let's begin learning what it takes for a person to truly thrive as they grow from baby to child and even on through adulthood.

Dr. Wilder's thriving chart illustrates what it takes to thrive, what the opposite of thriving is and the area of the brain that is involved in thriving. This chart is an overview to which I will speak more specifically as we go. The first four areas of the brain involved are on the right side, the side for emotions and relationships. The last area brings in the left side of the brain where words and logic reside. These five centers are designed to work together—to be synchronized—for thriving.

WHAT DOES IT TAKE TO THRIVE?

THRIVING	NOT THRIVING	BRAIN LEVEL
1) Belonging	Insecure Attachment	The Attachment Center (Thalamus) **Who or what is important to me?**
2) Receiving & giving life.	Self-centered	The Evaluation Center (Amygdala) **What is Good, Bad, Scary?**
3) Synchronizing, Return-to-joy, Forgiveness	Loss of Synchronization	The "Mother Core" (Cingulate) **Peace, Joy, Distress**
4) Maturity	Immaturity	The Joy Center (Pre-frontal-cortex) **My identity and attention to the World**
5) Knowing My Heart	Living by the Flesh	The Logic Center (Left and Right Hemispheres together) **My explanations of my life**

I want to take a moment and look briefly at the "Thriving" versus "Not Thriving" sections of each component of this chart in order to get a better understanding of each part. I've included a little scenario with each one to help you get a better handle on their meanings:

BELONGING VERSUS INSECURE ATTACHMENTS

As most of us know, the basis for life is a place to belong. Wanting to belong is universal and desired by every human, bringing much emotional pain when not a part of life. In our deepest being we know "who is important to us," and to whom we want to be important. As we go through our study here, we will see the benefits of a secure attachment from birth and the pain and destruction that come from feeling that we do not belong.

At birth and immediately after, infants want to bond with their parents. These are the most important bonds. But belonging is so important that all of us need many loving bonds at every age and stage of life. Dr. Wilder talks about both. "In the bonds we form with parents we see who we are as if looking in a mirror. Because those mirrors are imperfect, we need a loving community of bonds to fill in the gaps." (p. 56 *The Life Model*) Because of the faulty mirror, this means that all of us need lots of people in our lives who will love, cherish and care for us. None of us can have too many loving attachments. And the principle loving attachment we all need is God's family, because without Him there is no true life. When we receive His Son, the Lord Jesus, God adopts us into His family with a secure and loving bond. (If you are not certain that you have a personal relationship with Jesus, talk to a trusted friend for help.)

Daniel

Daniel grew up in a foster home where the foster parents took care of his needs, but did not consistently connect with him emotionally. They were very busy with their own interests, sometimes giving Daniel attention, sometimes not. Daniel was constantly looking for someone to make him feel better. Now an adult, Daniel has a difficult time relating to other people, although he has married and has a family. The insecurity he felt from his deep loneliness causes him to feel jealous when his wife does activities on her own. He wants her to be around as much as possible. Daniel has many fears about his abilities, his finances, and his future because he feels so needy. He is unable to trust God and is afraid to take the risk that God might not be able to help him. Because Daniel did not experience a secure attachment growing up, neediness rules his life.

RECEIVING AND GIVING LIFE VERSUS SELF-CENTERED

As I hope you noted in this second heading from the Thrive chart, receiving and giving life is reversed from the way we usually think about it. We must receive (emotionally or physically) *before* we can give. We are dependent on God for each and every breath. If we try to give before we receive, whether it is emotional support, leading at work or helping others, we will burn out. There will not be a good foundation from which to give. It might look like we are interested in others when, in reality, we may be looking to feel important and valuable because of the giving. On the other hand, if we only receive and seldom give, we will consume everything for ourselves. Both of these extremes turn the focus to self instead of others.

Every moment God demonstrates the opposite of self-centeredness as He constantly pours out His grace and mercy upon us. Receiving life first from Him and having strong relationships with others builds a good foundation for giving. God's perfect love casts out fear; one of the principle factors in self-centeredness, and replaces fear with His deep, need-meeting love. (I John 4:18) We must connect with God and look to Him to fill us with those characteristics we need to relate well with others and to be able to live in love instead of fear.

Jessica

· *Jessica is very unhappy and worried most of the time, though few people can see it, because Jessica tries to be" invisible" wherever she is. Jessica grew up with a father who hit her mother when he was upset. Jessica was the parent at home, a task that she was not built to carry. As Jessica grew to adulthood, it remained very difficult for her to live life, as she had not received enough life herself. Having to give without receiving enough first has formed Jessica into a person with lots of fear and worry. The foundation for her self-image is very shaky. It is difficult for her to relate authentically, because of growing up in an environment full of addictions and abuse. As an adult, Jessica will not say what she thinks for fear of being rejected. Because of the responsibility that she carried so young, at church she is the first to volunteer, but will not let anyone know when she herself is in need. Jessica tries to give without receiving first.*

SYNCHRONIZING/RECOVERY VERSUS LOSS OF SYNCHRONIZATION

Because synchronization is so important to what I desire to get across here, we will take more than one chapter to look at it. We will look at how synchronizing affects bonding, peace, joy and distress. Understanding synchronization maximizes thriving, whether we are speaking of synchronizing in our hearts with God, within ourselves, within the brain, or with others. Synchronizing—matching energy and being in tune with—on the same page with another—is vital in all relating. When we synchronize with another, they feel valuable, special and loved.

The opposite happens with long-term or early loss of synchronization. That kind of de-synchronization can be traumatic and the person then must find recovery from traumas in order to reach maximum growth. Recovery involves embracing all the pain in our lives and allowing God to heal us. We work through our own pain and help others with theirs. As we build joy strength from those who are glad to be with us, we find peace in the healing and learn how to handle distress. (p. 36 *The Life Model*) Relating through a model of synchronizing joy, peace and recovery from distress can prevent traumas and build strength into all of us that will undergird us in times of distress.

Kaleb

Kaleb appears to be a person without problems. As a young child, his mother stayed busy and seldom paid attention to him when he needed her. This hurt deeply so he pretended not to care. If asked he will say he had a good childhood. Through the years, Kaleb has grown into a person who tries to control people around him. If he tries to be in a relationship, he does not know how to connect with what the other person is feeling. Others report he is aloof and unemotional. When there is conflict, Kaleb withdraws and will not talk because he does not know how to recover from a disruption in the relationship. Kaleb finds it very difficult to handle distress and connect with others.

MATURITY VERSUS IMMATURITY

We have already looked at maturity in the last chapter as a vital part of healthy development. One way we defined maturity was "reaching one's God given potential." Maturity grows best in real, joy-filled relationships. In the following chapters we will look closer at the importance of joy strength as the basis for reaching maturity. Joy strength means to have enough joy in one's life to offset distressing circumstances. Handling distress well is one sign of maturity.

There is an area of the brain that interacts and functions through joy. Although many places in a baby's brain reach an end to their growth during the first few months, the Joy Center in the brain never stops growing as we interact in loving bonds throughout life. As we said in Chapter Two, the community of loving relationships helps us reach our full capabilities. (pp. 15-16 *The Life Model*) Having maturity as one of our personal goals can help us with periodic check-ups as we determine how we are progressing. Knowing how joy fits into the equation will insure a strong foundation for the path to maturity.

Veronica

Veronica almost never does anything except what she wants to do. She expects everyone to know what she wants and gets upset when they don't. She thinks being liked and having the right things will make her happy, so she spends every penny she gets in her hands. If anyone crosses Veronica, she pouts or whines or blows up. It is very hard for her to calm down if she doesn't get her way. Veronica did not have very much joy built into her life growing up and her parents did not discipline her at all. She did not learn delay of gratification, empathy for others or how to come to compromise in a relationship. Now when she should be acting as an adult, Veronica is stuck in the Child stage.

Vanessa

On the other hand, Vanessa is a well-adjusted adult who maintains her relationships with her family and friends even when there are upsets and conflicts. She is able to work through problems without blowing up or withdrawing. She is a stable influence with her children, keeping a fairly good balance of taking care of herself while giving to them without expecting anything in return. Vanessa knows what she likes and who she is, and thus she is not afraid to discuss issues with those around her and compromise when necessary. Vanessa is willing to do her part and feels free to speak her mind even though someone might disagree with her. Vanessa grew up understanding some of the consequences that come with not living God's way and was willing to adjust her choices accordingly. Along with a foundation built on God, Vanessa's parents gave her a foundation for thriving by building lots of joy into her life (and brain) during the early years of her life. As an adult, Vanessa is not perfect, but her stability and her commitment to staying relational even during intense emotions have taken her in the right direction. Vanessa has earned the Adult stage and entered the Parent stage.

KNOWING MY HEART VERSUS LIVING BY THE FLESH

We get to know our heart from input of those around us who truly know us and see us through Heaven's eyes; those who see us the way God sees us. If we have not been told correctly who we are, we will not be able to walk out what we talk. We will have faulty explanations of life and live from lies instead of truth. We will try to get our love and acceptance from the wrong places. When we receive Jesus into our hearts, we can learn to live from His guidance and see life as He does, and we will know the truth that our love and acceptance come from Him. As we grow with Jesus, we will be less likely to listen to old beliefs that were part of our past that do not fit us. As we live from God's perspective we can walk what we talk.

Will

Will is a leader in his church. Most of the church members think Will is the model Christian. But they do not see Will when he is out and about with his buddies. Will's walk does not match his talk because he is looking for acceptance in the wrong places. Although he is a Christian, Will does not know how God sees and accepts him. Like a chameleon, Will changes according to what he thinks others want him to be. One of the reasons Will struggles is because his parents always expected him to be perfect and then put him down when he was not. They did not do a good job of providing a safe place for Will to make mistakes and fail. Their focus was on what Will did instead of who God had made him to be. Living with perfectionism instead of acceptance has influenced Will to act like a different person depending on whom he is with. Will lives out many lies hidden in his heart about who he really is.

# # # #

SYNCHRONIZATION

After looking at the five ingredients for thriving and these scenarios to illustrate each one, let's go a step further and look at how healthy development in a person's life fits with the way God has designed our brains to synchronize with Him, with each other and with ourselves. In the introduction to this section, synchronization was defined as "being on the same page as another and sharing energy levels." Although it may be a new term, understanding the importance of synchronizing and doing it are basic to joy-filled relationships. We will continue to use this word in the following chapters and I highly encourage you to make this word part of your vocabulary, to come to understand it and to *do* it, as a vital way of relating to everyone.

Synchronization is one of the most important foundations for thriving because it is the basis for a secure attachment. In the next chapter we will look more closely at how a mother's ability to "read the baby" insures that she will build good hardwiring into her infant as they interact in joy and quiet. The mother's ability to synchronize actually affects the growing brain and its emotional stability. As we go through this study, we want to notice our own ability to "read others" and synchronize with them. It is never too late to learn to synchronize and build secure bonds.

As you will see shortly, the Joy Center (where joy building takes place in the brain) eventually becomes 35% of the adult brain. Like our computers, we want the hardware (the brain) to run efficiently so that the software will work. The software, the goals we want for ourselves, all have to do with relationships in some form or another. Relating healthily is the basis of all that software. If we grew up with a mother who did not synchronize well, our ability to relate well may have been affected. In Chapter Three we will see more clearly how the lack of synchronization affects bonding, which affects how we relate to others, to God and to ourselves.

As we begin to truly synchronize with others, being on the same wave length and matching their energy level, whether it is with our spouses, children or friends, relating changes in a very positive way. When we synchronize, we communicate unconditional love and acceptance; we communicate caring; we communicate that the other person is important. Synchronizing and being glad to be together are how others "get it." There is a message sent that says something like, "I can put myself aside here and focus on you and where you are at this moment. You are so important." Anytime I am feeling low, the person I want to talk to is someone who knows how to synchronize. I might want to hear some truth, but usually after I've first had some empathy in the form of synchronizing. I like it when another person meets me in my distress right where I am and does not try to "fix" me quickly just so he or she will feel better.

In *Living With Men*, Dr. Wilder compares synchronization to good music. He calls synchronizing, "the emotional equivalent of good music: timing, intensity and tone." We all know how beautiful a guitar sounds when it is played with good timing, correct intensity and right tone. We recognize a familiar song and enjoy its harmony. Not only does harmony sound good, it feels good to our whole body. We feel quite the opposite when we hear an instrument out of synchronization, with bad timing, intensity and tone. We feel our skin crawl and our teeth grate.

After learning about the importance of synchronizing, I realized that there are times when we do not synchronize by being overly jubilant when someone else is sitting quietly with a low level of energy. It can be easy to do with a child when we feel that surge of love for him and then swoop down upon him to give a big hug when he is playing quietly. Giving big hugs when someone is quiet is not really synchronizing, because the timing is not good. The motive and desire were great, but the timing was jarring.

Like making good music, we learn to synchronize by doing it with someone who knows how. We can find the ideal that God has designed for learning this skill by looking at what is supposed to happen the first year of life. Mothers are supposed to teach their children to synchronize by synchronizing with them. Synchronizing helps the baby learn how to deal with distress and the brain itself grows correctly. The good mother uses proper timing, intensity and tone by matching the baby's timing, intensity and tone. It is vital and good only when *the mother synchronizes with the baby, watching to see when baby needs to rest after building joy.* (In the next chapter we will go into detail about building joy and resting.) The mother, as the older brain, "leads" by watching and knowing when to allow rest. It is not good, and is in fact damaging, if the mother tries to get the baby to match her needs of wanting connection.

The process of building joy and allowing rest by matching energy begins as soon as the baby can focus his eyes. We all need good synchronization skills for our whole lifetime, and the foundation is laid early between mother and baby as they interact face to face. Most everyone enjoys playing "goo-goo," getting the baby to smile and then laugh as we smile and speak that silly language. In this playing joy with its accompanying baby talk, what we don't consciously realize is that we are communicating non-verbally, back and forth, eye to eye. Although it is not really noticeable, this communication is taking place left eye to left eye. The communication is going on between the mother's right brain and the baby's right brain at a subconscious level. They are synchronizing joy, which is affecting the brain positively, when done correctly, by allowing rest when the baby reaches her peak of joy.

Right about now you might be wondering why all the detail about babies. Isn't this a relationship book for adults? The answer to that question is vital: adults who did not get what they needed as babies need to learn to play "goo-goo" as adults. That is what this book is about. In a safe, joy-filled community, neglect and abuse have to be replaced with trust and joy. Good stories have to be told, appreciation learned and safe bonds built that are not sexualized. People have to grieve what they did not get and see that it is not too late to prevent passing negatives on to their children. So please keep reading.

Brenna in high joy—three months old

Where do timing, intensity and tone come in? When done correctly, the mother and baby are synchronizing joy and quietness. In a good situation, the mother matches the baby's intensity of joy, watching for when he has reached his peak of joy so that she can let him quiet (rest) at that proper timing. The mother synchronizes the tone (joy) of the encounter according to how much joy and quiet the *baby* desires. In good synchronization, and in good parenting, the baby's needs are monitored in this process and a good mother stays "in tune" with her baby's needs. The mother leads in the sense that she watches the baby's need to connect or rest, but the baby's needs are the determining factor. This dance of synchronization is all about building joy and allowing the baby to rest in between, and it is the basis for wiring up the hardware (brain) the whole first year of life.

Connor and Jodi synchronize joy, left eye to left eye

As the mother and baby smile at each other, the joy increases and they climb higher in intensity, until the mother senses that the baby is at his peak, and she backs off to let him rest. Then when he is ready, usually just a few seconds, they build joy again. Whatever emotion is going on in the right side of the brain of each person shows up in each one's left eye. *Six complete cycles* of interaction pass back and forth between both the mother and the baby in one second, too quickly for conscious thought—but the interactions through their eyes are having an effect. These cycles take place below conscious level and cannot be faked. If some other emotion besides joy is going on in the mother, this is what will show up in her left eye. Because this joy and quiet (or other emotions) cannot be faked, baby is affected by what she sees on the other face. What baby sees will be the mirror in which she builds her self- image. The best self-image building and brain hardwiring are done with joy!

Erica (15) synchronizes perfectly with Ryan (8 months)

So what if the mother is not synchronizing, watching for rest, being on the same page and matching energy with her baby? This is de-synchronizing. De-synchronization, the opposite of good synchronization is like bad timing, intensity and tone in music. Upon hearing a musical discord, we can hardly bear more than a few seconds of the noise. De-synchronization feels the same way on an emotional level. De-synchronization happens when an encounter between an adult and baby or child (or another adult) is about the adult's needs instead of the baby or child's (or other adult's). A stranger, or even an unfamiliar relative, might approach a baby with a big smile, wanting to "play joy." Quite often the baby does not respond with a smile and maybe draws back. Bad synchronization increases the intensity by perhaps reaching out to touch the baby and get her to play, pressing her to perform. In de-synchronization, the baby's needs are not monitored and he feels the discord that we feel upon hearing the out-of-tune guitar. A bad "mother/adult" tries to get the baby to meet "her" needs. The following picture of Kori (age 1) and a stranger cousin is an example of this de-synchronization.

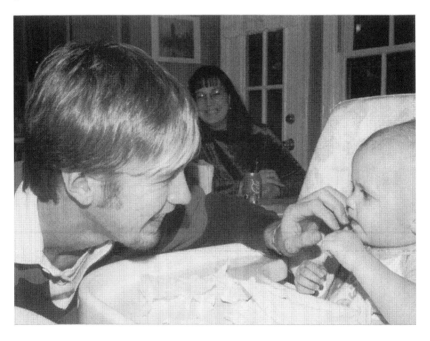

Cousin Bronzie "presses" Kori to respond

Although Bronzie is a cousin, Kori did not know him and she was not sure about playing joy with a stranger. A temporary press from a stranger is not damaging, as it would be from a caretaker who relates in a de-synchronized manner day in and day out. De-synchronization is not good mothering and when we look at bonding we will see what results can happen from not synchronizing.

　　　　　　　　　　　　© 2012 Barbara Moon

As a good mother interacts and synchronizes with her baby, over time the baby learns what to do with emotional distress, those moments when he is stretched to the limit and needs to rest. He learns how to stay synchronized in the relationship while mother helps him calm, because she does not overwhelm him. As the pair practices building joy and quiet together, the emotional control center in the brain learns how to get back to peace and joy from uneasy emotions, and very soon the baby knows how to self-calm. When the baby is older, around twelve months, mother will teach him to return to joy from more distressing emotions than he is equipped to handle the first year.

It is important to note that this skill of knowing when to back off and not overwhelm someone is passed down physically through this right-brain to right-brain synchronization or de-synchronization. We download to others what we have. We received what our mothers had unless we have downloaded from someone else along the way. We either know how to do the joy building and backing off to rest or we don't. It depends on the bond we had with our mother and the training we practiced that first year with her. But please continue if that frightens you, because these techniques can be learned. Adults can "download" to other adults; it just takes more time and practice. And that is why I am passionate about giving you this somewhat technical information—first because we can prevent problems when done early, and secondly, it's possible to do remedial work later on, as we will see in the Appendix exercises.

# # # #

Now let's look at how the emotional areas of the brain fit into the thriving chart from which we took the "life and death" opposites. The chart shows five brain levels and these five levels need to stay synchronized with each other in order for us to thrive, to be able to synchronize with others, and to be able to handle distress. Let's consider the five levels again as being somewhat like our computers. Most of us know how windows work in a computer, how more than one can be opened at a time. We also understand how frustrating it is when something on the computer is not functioning properly. Let's suppose we are working on a project where we need five windows open at the same time. One window is central for the top two and the bottom two to function. A problem arises in the middle window that causes the top two to shut down. Now the project is on hold and cannot operate properly just with the two bottom windows. All these windows are de-synchronized. This is a very simple analogy of the five levels and how they need to be synchronized for any of us to relate well. We will look at the five levels separately and then together.

This section is very important for understanding the basis of the brain science and relating well with others. Since it is a little technical and has new terms, I have interspersed pictures and stories to illustrate the points and make them easier to grasp. But you do not have to know the names of the brain parts or where they are located in order to be able to bond, build joy and quiet and synchronize. The information will simply give some detail and clarity to reasons why we have relationship problems when our brain de-synchronizes when we are overwhelmed. This chapter, along with Chapters Three and Four are foundational and will detail bonding, joy and returning to joy, all of which are relationship skills that we need to understand regardless of our age.

THE EMOTIONAL CONTROL CENTER

We now begin a more detailed look at the emotional control center of the brain in the Right Hemisphere. For the five centers or levels, I will give each a name and a number. In later chapters we will most often speak of the levels by their number. **The Attachment Center (Level 1)** is the deepest level in the control center where bonding takes place, beginning at birth. We will look closely at bonding in a later section. You may remember this center as part of the thriving chart where Daniel was lonely and unable to trust God because of his insecurities. He did not have a secure bond. This level tells us who or what is important to us. The scientific name for the Attachment Center (Level 1) is the *thalamus,* a deep, sub-conscious area of the brain that actually lights up on brain scans which the brain researchers are now using. The "attachment light" comes on when we want to draw close and goes off when we want to be alone. When there is a certain person that we want to be with, only that one person will do. We often say we are missing that person if unable to connect with them.

Missing someone causes us emotional pain. Here in the brain's Attachment Center, we feel our deepest joys and deepest pains which we call A*ttachment Pain.* Attachment Pain is the worst kind of pain we can feel; the kind of horrendous pain we feel when someone dies or a divorce happens. We experience a milder form when someone is on a long trip and we miss him or her. We feel Attachment Pain whenever we want to connect with someone and can't, regardless of the circumstances that may be preventing the connection. We feel very alone. Later we will look at how *avoiding* Attachment Pain causes addictions and is very detrimental to mental health and thriving.

This Attachment Center (Level 1) is where we build relationships. Here babies develop what is called an "internal interpreter," the ability to know what the person he is bonded with is thinking. We carry this ability with us into adulthood so that we "know" others very well. The ability to know what a bonded person thinks will continue to function even after the bonded person is dead. We all know what our mothers would think about certain things whether she is living or not.

In addition to the internal interpreter, the capacity we have to synchronize with others and the ability to repair broken attachments are in the Attachment Center. When we look at the section on bonding, we will see how these two fit together. When we know how to repair ruptures (disconnects that result from conflict) in our relationships, we do not fear having a rupture. This makes the disconnection easier because we know we will get back together (return to joy). In relationships there will be ruptures; they are inevitable. Knowing how to repair ruptures frees us from performance based acceptance and worry about having conflicts. The rupture and repair cycle are the key to relationships, not the avoidance of conflict.

Because the Attachment Center in the brain is below conscious level, it is always on and does not shut down during distress, as do some of the higher levels of the brain. Because it is always running, it is very important for this area of the brain to be strong and have steady, loving bonds with others. There will never be any human who does not need other people even if they pretend to be all right alone or seem to be self-sufficient. Secure attachments are foundational for healthy emotions.

The Evaluation Center (Level 2), also on the right side of the brain and the next deepest level of the control center, is technically called the *amygdale*. Dr. Wilder affectionately calls it our "guard shack," because it warns us when to fight or to flee. This area develops from pre-birth to two months. It responds all through life to the training it receives about what is good, bad, and/or scary, telling us what to approach or avoid, what is life-giving or not life-giving. You will remember the story for the thriving chart of Jessica who was afraid of her daddy, took on too much responsibility and who worried all the time. Jessica's Evaluation Center, Level 2, had learned to keep her in a state of fear.

As Level 2 is programmed with what is good, bad, or scary, that is what the person will believe about that event, object, or person. Although what we believe about an event, object or person being good, bad or scary may not be the truth, whatever the Evaluation Center believes about it, that's what it will operate when Level 2 is in control, whenever the higher brain levels shut down. Not wanting to be run by fear is another reason for keeping the five levels of the brain synchronized. When the Evaluation Center (Level 2) is in control, all of life is about fear and the person lives from that fear base, tracking his or her environment with fear. A child in school who is living from a fear base will have a difficult time focusing on class work. He will subconsciously be watching his environment for things that are bad and scary. His attention will not be on the teacher, as it needs to be, and his classroom performance will show it. Adults living from fear will be controlling, will not be able to rest and will not feel safe, pushing others away who get too close or clinging to them unhealthily.

The Evaluation Center (Level 2) functions non-verbally, getting programmed by responses from the body. What it believes about good, bad, and scary *cannot be overcome by the will and it never changes its opinions.* There is a way to overcome what it has learned, but we will see that later. The guard shack is not logical and can never be reasoned with. It never forgets what it has learned, and like the Attachment Center (Level 1), it is always on, never shut down, ready to take over automatically when distress overwhelms the brain and shuts down the three upper levels listed below.

Because of these attributes often based on fears, the Evaluation Center (Level 2) is Satan's favorite place to program, since it will continuously broadcast to the rest of the brain what is bad and scary, thus shutting down the upper levels and causing de-synchronization to occur. It causes the person to use fear to motivate others and tracks in fear if so trained. When people know how to avoid traumas that cause fears, get healing from their past traumas or know how to quickly repair present traumas, instead of living from fear, they live with a strong sense of security and find it easier to trust God and handle distress. They enjoy better relationships.

Perhaps you can identify with my earliest memory of bad and scary. When I was about four years old, my mother took me to the dentist for the first time. In those days, the dentists did not give painkillers when they drilled. I experienced great pain more than once as a dentist drilled and filled my decayed baby teeth. To this day, I hate going to the dentist and I feel great anxiety even when my mouth is full of Novocain. I cannot choose for this fear to go away. But thanks to God, who designed the brain, there is a way to calm the Evaluation

Center (Level 2) and after many years of practicing that calming, I can now go somewhat adult-like to the dentist.

An incident happened with my granddaughters, Kayli and Kori, the twins with whom I used to live, which can illustrate how dealing quickly with a fear avoids a trauma. One evening when they were almost two, the twins and I were in the bathroom getting ready for their bath. Tyler, who was in Kindergarten, opened the door to proudly show off a little paper mask that she had made at school that day. When the twins saw an odd-looking bear's face peeking and growling at them through the now opened door, they immediately screamed in terror. They had never seen a mask and had no idea what was growling at them right there in the bathroom. I quickly told Tyler to remove the mask so they could see it was she and after a few minutes I was able to calm both twins. Then we took time to look at the mask while I held them and helped them to face this new thing that had caused so much terror. As we synchronized, calmed and observed the mask, we quickly repaired what could have been a "trauma." I did not want them to be afraid of masks the rest of their life.

The **Mother Core (Level 3),** the *cingulate*, is the third level of the emotional brain. It is in the middle of the control center. I am calling it the "Mother Core," since this is what much of the scientific literature calls it. From this part of the brain, mothers literally download their Mother Core into that part of their new baby's brain. This takes place during the second to ninth months and is associated with all the time spent synchronizing and building joy and quiet, as the two interact left eye to left eye while building their bond. The Mother Core enables the two brains to match energy states (synchronize). Dr. Wilder says in

Living With Men, "The mother's older brain duplicates itself in her baby, including what mother knows and how her brain is built."[5] Level 3 synchronizes the different lobes of the brain, the upper and lower levels of the control center, and baby and mommy's Mother Cores with each other. (pp. 39-40 *Living With Men*) When the Mother Core functions as it was designed, synchronizing the lower and higher places in the control center, the person thrives. Feeling overwhelmed will shut off Level 3—and now Level 2 will take over as described above. Fear will run the show.

The Mother Core (Level 3) is also the part of the brain that understands personal space, tracks eye movements, enables us to dance, and knows empathy. It is the place that produces a true joy smile, not a smile that says "cheese" for the camera.

Brenna has a joy smile

Brenna and Aaron say 'cheese'

At about five months of age, babies' brains are able to discern that there is another mind behind the face at which they are looking. This is called "mind-sight." Babies become like the faces with which they are

---

[5] E. James Wilder, *Living With Men*, Shepherd's House, Inc., Pasadena, CA, 2004; www.lifemodel.org

synchronizing, copying the mother's brain (or principle caretaker's). They learn who they are from the reflection of that other face and whether their world is bounded by joy or fear. The caretakers pass on what they have in their Mother Core. They cannot pretend to have something they don't have nor try to pass on something they wish they had. Kaleb, from our chart stories, resigned himself to not having his mother synchronize well with him and learned to pretend he was all right.

But there is good news—*the **Mother Core can be improved!*** Synchronizing with a person who has a stronger Mother Core than you have will grow that part of your brain. But it will take tons more time and energy than when done at the proper time at the age of two to nine months. Although it can take many years of counseling or mentoring, one on one, to grow a better Mother Core, it can be done. It takes a strong bond and the willingness to work through difficult issues, trusting God for healing and growth. It takes courage to admit we need help and to find a mentor who will download their brain into ours.

Another function of the Mother Core is that it is the emotional bond for *two* faces. It can synchronize with only *one other* at a time. It can think about others, but it can only synchronize with one other at a time. The two people synchronize joy, quiet or distress. In a later chapter we will look closely at joy, quiet and calming distress.

Which one is synchronizing real joy?

Learning that we can only synchronize with one person at a time is very helpful living in a family or being in a community or a group. It helps explain how we feel pulled in different directions like a ping-pong ball bouncing back and forth, especially during conflict. Trying to synchronize with more than one can cause us to feel overwhelmed, which will de-synchronize the brain, causing us to lose our maturity and make matters worse. We can deal with more than one if we are able to stay calm and mature, but it will take a little longer to go back and forth.

A few years ago, when Tyler, the oldest was about six, I had an exceptionally colorful lesson about only being able to synchronize with one other at a time. The girls and I were in the van on a hot summer day, hooking car seats and belts, in preparation for a trip to the grocery store. Have you ever been in a van with four little girls under the age of six, when a bee buzzed into the van? I don't think I have ever heard so

70   © 2012 Barbara Moon

much screaming, yelling and crying in my life. It was very difficult to calm this ocean of distress by myself as I frantically shooed at the bee while trying to use my voice to calm the girls. It felt like an hour went by before I got the bee out of the van and could one by one, back and forth, calm the screaming girls enough to continue our trip to the store. Interacting in a large family will always feel like a ping-pong match, but it becomes easier as we realize staying calm and going back and forth will work, it just takes a little longer to get to calm.

Intense distress, such as bees in a van or conflict between two or more people, can be overwhelming to any of us. When distress overwhelms our joy capacity to handle distress, the brain de-synchronizes. I call it *a meltdown*. We are supposed to learn from our mothers what to do during overwhelming distress. What we need is the same throughout our lifetime. We need to find someone with a brain that is greater (more mature) than ours to help us calm in the midst of the overwhelm. Finding a bigger brain is not always a conscious search, depending on the height of the intensity. And finding help can be more complex with adults who have not learned to receive—or ask—for what they need. If we grew up not getting validation and comfort when upset, we will not know how to get it—or receive it—as an adult. It's important to know when we need help because we need to find peace before we can solve a problem. And more importantly, we *will* bond with whoever calms us.

The greater mind we turn to during overwhelming distress can be God's. His mind is always greater and always available to us any time we turn to Him. He is the peace for which we are longing. Wise is the person who knows when his/her capacity is overwhelmed and can ask

God or someone else for help. In a mature and strongly bonded relationship, adults can be each other's "greater mind" during intense emotions, when one is able to synchronize with the other and both have not "melted down" at the same time.

Besides searching for a greater mind to help in need, another function of the Mother Core is the ability to detect when someone is lying to us. This is because the interchanges going back and forth in the left eyes are six times per second, below conscious thought. When looking eye-to-eye and synchronizing, we cannot fake what is going on inside our minds. This is why people who are lying look down or away. Perhaps a trained CIA agent or a hardened criminal might be able to hide their true feelings eye to eye, but most of us cannot.

All of the Mother Core's brain-synchronizing functions, including synchronizing the upper and lower levels of the brain's control center, are done by joy between the two bonded faces. So what happens when joy is not the emotion going on between the two? We will look more closely at this scenario in a later chapter, but for now let's see what is lost when a negative emotion overwhelms the Mother Core and causes a meltdown. The de-synchronization, or meltdown, shuts down the top two layers that we have not looked at yet—the **Logic Center (Level 5)** and the **Joy Center (Level 4)**. Now the Attachment Center and the Evaluation Center, those below consciousness, will run the brain, or person, automatically. Relational circuits are off and this is not good, as we looked at before, because now *fear* will be the motivator of all that is going on with the person since the Evaluation Center (Level 2) is running the show. What is supposed to be motivating us? Joy, peace and love—*not fear*. As we look at what functions occur in the Logic and Joy Centers, we will see that very important life and relational skills are missing when these Centers are shut down. We want to keep the Mother Core (Level 3) running, because it determines how the brain stays synchronized. *How Level 3 runs and stays running is determined by the level of joy the person has.*

The Joy Center (Level 4), the fourth center on the right side of the brain that we want to consider, is called the Right Pre-fontal Cortex and is located in the upper front part of the brain in the Right Hemisphere, behind the right eye. It develops in the first 24 months of life, becoming 35% of the adult brain. The Joy Center is the place where joy is built. Joy is so important to thriving that I will spend a whole chapter on it. We want to build and maintain lots of joy in order to train and keep this part of the brain running, because lack of joy capacity in this area will greatly affect moral and social behavior. When it goes off, we lose our maturity, we become non-relational, we cannot hear words and we do not act like ourselves.

Here in the Joy Center we also have our impulse control and goal directed behavior, functions that are vital to joy-filled relationships and living life. Remember Veronica and Vanessa? Their different foundations of joy strength and capacity to handle distress greatly affected their maturity and how they responded to the complexities in their world.

The Joy Center also carries our personal preferences, gives us creativity and personal identity, does emotional regulation and determines what we will pay attention to in the world around us. The Joy Center (Level 4) enables us to switch the focus of our attention. If you stop to think about it, your attention is one of your most priceless commodities. Everyone wants your attention. This ability to focus and switch attention, as well as all the other functions of the Joy Center, are lost when there is not enough joy to keep the brain synchronized and functioning. We do not know what to do nor do we know what satisfies. In Chapter Eleven we will learn more about what satisfies.

In the Joy Center (Level 4), babies also carry an image of their mother's face that interprets the meaning of the baby's life. This message that the baby carries about life revolves around either joy or fear. Are you noting how what we have been looking at ties together? Joy or fear can be the building blocks for our lives. We learn the joy or fear message from *non-verbal* images and memories, not from words. In the chapter on joy, we will look at how joy is built non-verbally and re-emphasize the importance of lots of joy in everyone's life.

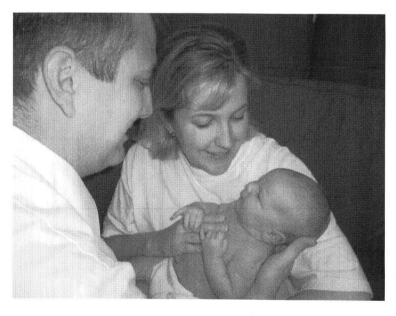

Three faces--Rick, Jodi and Connor (five days old)

Unlike the Mother Core (Level 3), which is a two-way focus, the Joy Center (Level 4) has room for a *third* face. It carries a three-way mental image of two people looking at each other while the third face watches. Ideally in the formation months, the three faces are baby, mother and father. To work as this part of the brain is designed, these three faces must be in joy. The child sees only from his or her perspective. He knows nothing about circumstances or problems going on in the adults. He simply records joy or fear (or anger). One reason this is important is that it affects the baby's view of God. If for example mother and baby are in joy and the baby looks to the third face (Daddy) and he is scowling, the brain can be programmed to think this is the way God is. When baby looks at daddy and his face is enjoying baby and mother's joy, the baby feels secure. He will get a realistic "picture" of God. (***See Appendix—Chapter Three—Triad Discussion 2)***

Throughout life, we are able to continue three-way bonds when the Joy Center is functioning. The three in the bond might be two friends and God, three friends, three family members, etc. In addition, when the Joy Center (Level 4) is running well, we can have three points of view. Having three points of view is very useful, because the three-way focus in the Joy Center provides the means to calm the fear in the Evaluation Center (Level 2) and override its opinions of bad and scary. *Validation of emotions* and *comfort* are two necessary ingredients for this override to occur. We will look further at both in Chapter Eight.

The Father's patience—Greg and Tyler—three-way focus

Here is how it works: Viewpoint one, the child's, sees or feels something scary. Viewpoint two, the adult's, decides how he or she will react to the scary situation. When the situation is not overwhelming to the adult, the adult synchronizes with the child, gives comfort and calms the distress. Now they can look at the scary and bad situation, object or feeling together while validating the feelings. Remember when I calmed everyone after the growling bear mask and then we looked at the mask? The older brain helps calm the distress in the younger brain and overrides the fear, bringing peace and quiet. Now the child/person will not experience a trauma because he or she has received comfort, synchronization and a different perspective on the fearful event or object. The bond will deepen between the two people, as all of us wants to be with those who calm us. The three-way focus for calming and avoiding a trauma works in all relationships regardless of age. In Chapter Six we will study further how to calm the brain through body exercises and heal emotional wounds through the Immanuel Process. In Chapter Eight we will revisit the three-way bond.

Another way to look at the three-way focus is through imagining a classroom, a seminar, job training, or a family meeting between spouses. I cannot teach you anything nor have a good discussion until I get your attention. In the Joy Center, when all is functioning correctly, we are able to direct attention and bring the focus onto the lesson or topic at hand.

How joy was built in Level 4 during the first two years of life affects the coping abilities you have as an adult. Joy capacity greatly determines how you walk through life, how well you handle distress, and whether you shut down during intense emotions. When the brain is well trained and synchronized, a person will not shut down easily under distress, but will, as Dr. Wilder calls it, "suffer well." Suffering well means that we can continue to be relational and remember who we are, at whatever maturity level we have earned, during the distress. Below is a picture of Brenna, around the age of three, after I had just pierced one of her ears. Although she knows there is about to be some pain, she suffers well in Mommy's arms and keeps acting like herself.

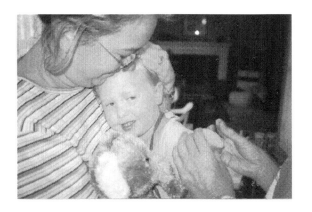

Brenna suffers well

The best example of suffering well is how Jesus behaved while on the Cross. Though His suffering was horrendous, both physically and emotionally, He continued to relate to those around Him and act like Himself. In Chapter One we mentioned the ability of emergency responders and other heroes to stay synchronized in high level stress, as they remain calm when many people would panic.

Suffering well happens when our joy capacity, a.k.a. our Joy Bucket, is at its fullest in the Joy Center (Level 4). This joy capacity grows best at the times that the brain is most receptive, between the second and ninth months of age, but the Joy Center (Level 4) is one of the few places in the emotional brain where growth continues throughout life. This makes retraining the Joy Center vital to helping those who did not receive the joy they needed as babies. Joy capacity can be built throughout the lifetime, but it will take longer to grow when not grown the first two years of life.

While remembering that building joy is important enough to have its own chapter, let's briefly recap the importance of building this Joy

Center regardless of a person's age. When running well, the Joy Center directs our attention to the world and joy keeps the whole brain synchronized with access to all functions. If overwhelmed by intense emotions, this joy part shuts down (Level 5 has already shut down), we lose our maturity and we cannot maintain our identity or act like ourselves. We've lost ourselves. We lose the ability to live from goal directed thinking, to maintain impulse control, to focus on tasks at hand, or remain calm during alarming situations. When the Joy Center (Level 4) shuts down we cannot calm the Evaluation Center (Level 2) and regulate distressing, fearful emotions. This affects moral and social behavior. We can no longer hear instructions. Words do not help. We need help from someone who is not overwhelmed by the distress, who can synchronize with us and bring us back to peace.

The Logic Center (Level 4+ or Level 5) is what I call the fifth area of the brain at which we want to look. (This level has been called both 4+ and 5. They are the same thing.) It is the left side of the pre-frontal cortex located in the Left Hemisphere or left side of the brain. When it is up and running, the Logic Center is the place for language and telling autobiographical stories. It is the place for explaining our lives. Like its name, it is the place for logic, reasoning and words. The Logic Center (Level 5) works best at school, seminars and listening to sermons and is not interested in helping us out much where negative emotions are concerned. If the negative emotions become too overwhelming, the Logic Center (Level 5) is the first area to shut down.

The Logic Center is the first level to shut down (de-synchronize) when distress overwhelms the person's capacity for joy in the Joy Center. In other words, the amount of joy we have determines the level of distress we can handle. The lack of access to Level 5, The Logic Center, causes confusion and the inability to walk what we talk. When the Logic Center is not functioning because of a meltdown, counseling, preaching, teaching, exhorting and admonishing fall on deaf ears—a deaf, de-synchronized brain. Words do not help a person who has a non-functioning Level 5; therefore, it is useless to lecture and instruct at that time. If we are in conflict with another person, it is useless to try to discuss a problem and reach a solution if Level 5 is off. Someone has to sit with the overwhelmed person, synchronize with the distress and calm the distress before the person can hear instructions. The meltdown problem cannot be fixed by words. Voice tone may help, but not words.

When the brain stays synchronized from the **Attachment Center (Level 1)** all the way to the **Logic Center (Level 5)**, the story is very different. When the brain is synchronized and running well we live from a coherent identity that is the same over time. We understand that we are the same person through the years and we act the same and have the same values regardless of distress. Remember Will who lived a dual life? He was not able to walk what he talked and did not have a consistent identity. This young man did not live from his heart, but rather lived from the lies that others had told him about himself.

When all levels of the control center are synchronized, we live by our heart. We Christians call the heart *our spirit*, which is the "eyes and ears" of the real us. After receiving Christ, the Holy Spirit lives in our spirit and leads us through our heart as we listen and obey His guidance. Living from the heart is the opposite of living by the "flesh," (*sark* in the Greek). The flesh is the "old programming and lies" that we received growing up. (Galatians 5:16) When we live by the flesh or *sark*, we lean on our own understanding instead of trusting in God. (Proverbs 3: 5 and 6)

Without healing, we are stuck with the old programming and lies from our childhood because the Logic Center (Level 5) does not change its opinions or beliefs that it has formed through the years. It will resist changes *even in the face of evidence to the contrary*—unless things get upset inside. Think about when a person goes to war. Before going, he or she may not believe in God or want God to be part of their life. Upon facing the dangers of war, upset occurs and not wanting anything to do with God may quickly change. Similarly, when a child gets sick or someone has a car wreck, people often turn to God whom they have not acknowledged before the upset. Being upset allows the right side of the brain to decide that the Logic Center (Level 5) can change its opinion. Knowing this principle dealt a blow to my fear of "upsetness." I used to believe that "peace at all costs" was better than upset. Now I feel less threatened if upset occurs because I know that it will be easier for me or the other person to change something we believe that is not the truth. Knowing this fact also changed my opinion of giving lots of evidence to someone with whom I disagreed. I could save my breath by not trying to talk them into something their Logic Center could not hear.

When the Logic Center shuts down from de-synchronization, we also lose the ability to explain ourselves and make sense of our circumstances. We feel confused and experience an incoherent identity. We aren't able to focus as well. This creates internal conflict and we need help finding the truth about the situation. According to Dr. Daniel

Siegel, author of *The Developing Mind*, when the Logic Center is down, we also cannot tell a good concise story about our past. His research has shown that the ability to tell a concise story about our past will reveal which of the four attachment styles we have. (p. 112 *The Developing Mind*).[6] We will be looking at those four bonds in a later chapter also, but for now let's look at why being able to tell stories is important.

Stories help us make sense of our world as we talk about painful events and receive comfort and validation. We want to get good at telling stories—stories from our own past, stories about our people, stories about the current family, stories about God, and stories about our children when they were young. This is how we pass down our heritage. Story telling also helps the brain because we use both the left side of the brain (language and logic) and the right side (emotions and synchronizing).

A good way to begin telling stories to our children is with picture albums and videos. But use words to tell the stories, not just the videos. As we tell stories, our listeners learn what it is like "us and our people" (our heritage) to do under various circumstances. Children love stories and they love to ask questions. As we tell our own stories to illustrate a value or resolution to a problem, or as we use Bible stories, parables, and fables, listeners absorb the lessons we want to instill in them. If you feel that you do not have a good heritage, tell stories that illustrate how *not* to do things. Use those stories; age

---

[6] Daniel J. Siegel, M.D., *The Developing Mind*, The Guilford Press, New York, 1999.

appropriately, as examples of how you want your listener to do differently than you or your ancestors did.

Another reason for telling stories is that when bad things happen, telling a story about it helps prevent trauma. This is one of the ways that all of us make sense of what happened. We need to process both the event and the emotions involved. (Siegel, *Parenting from the Inside Out*)[7] Processing often takes the form of talking about the event and/or emotions over and over for a while, but it can also be helpful to act out what happened or use props to tell the story. Even as adults we can tell stories about past experiences that have never made sense in order to process the emotions connected to the event. Unresolved traumas, grief and loss interfere with thriving and relating. (Siegel) As we discuss a negative event and the emotions that were bad or scary, it is important to give comfort and to tell the truth about all of it. It will not help prevent a trauma if we untruthfully tell the person that something is "no big deal" when it may be a big deal to them. This is part of synchronizing.

A while back my son, Greg, and his friend, Mike, had an occasion to practice comforting and telling the truth about an emotional event. They took Greg's four girls and Mike's son to see the movie *Eight Below*. The dads had not previewed the movie and did not know there was a part that was shockingly scary to little kids. Kori and Brenna nearly jumped out of their seats when, in one scene, a large leopard seal suddenly leapt out of a whale carcass, loudly roaring to the accompaniment of blaring music. Quickly each daddy took one of the girls onto his lap, held them closely and comforted them until the scene

---

[7] Daniel J. Siegel, M.D., *Parenting From the Inside Out*, 2003

changed. For two days afterwards, Brenna wanted to tell her mommy all about the scene in the movie, especially at bedtime. Mommy (Chris) allowed her to process it as long as she needed to; while at the same time synchronizing and helping her to peace as she did so. If the parents had scoffed at or ignored the fear and said it was no big deal, they would not have been telling the truth. If they had called the girls, "baby" for feeling scared, or hurried them through the process, there would not have been any validation about the feelings of terror they'd had.

SUMMARY

I hope the brain science did not sound too confusing and technical to you, and that I was able to break it down. I encourage you to study enough to get the gist of its importance. Let's spread the information as much as we can about synchronizing, building joy, allowing quiet together and bonding. These building blocks work best to make a good foundation when they are done at God's designed window of opportunity from pre-birth to around the age of two. But if that window of opportunity has passed, we can do remedial work, though it will take longer than at the designated time. Keep in mind that none of us can do everything perfectly, so when you blow it, seek forgiveness and stay glad to be together. Talk about scary things that happen so that traumas won't settle into your emotions. Keep in mind that prevention takes much less energy than recovery, but re-training is possible.

CHAPTER FOUR: BONDING, SYNCHRONIZATION, JOY AND QUIET

Goal: to understand bonding and the synchronization of joy and quiet together

INTRODUCTION

As we looked at Dr. Wilder's chart for thriving along with the scenarios after each section, it was easier to see that healthy development requires synchronization, joy, peace and rest, and truth. We looked at the maturity stages that humans grow through in order for us to observe the responsibility of maturing. We have looked at the levels of the emotional control center in the brain and how these five levels need to be synchronized in order for a person to be healthy. Now I would like to take a brief journey through the Infant Stage of maturity in order to illustrate how bonding, synchronization, joy and quiet contribute to the ideal that God has designed for joy-filled relationships. The ideal will help you better understand some of the needs and tasks in the maturity chapter while helping you see Type A traumas, the **A**bsence of good things you were supposed to receive. Although it is painful to see what we did not get, it is the pre-requisite for healing and growth. We cannot fix a problem that we don't know we have.

It is likely that most readers did not get the ideal foundation, at the ideal time the brain was prepared for it; therefore, we all need encouragement that remedial work can be done even though it takes more time and energy than when done during the first two years. As Dr. Wilder tells us how secure bonding, full joy capacity, synchronization, and God's truth are essential to a healthy life, we want to look at how well the first three essentials fit with how God designed the brain. We will look at Dr. Wilder's fourth requirement for healthy development—truth—in Chapter Nine—and sprinkled throughout the book.

BONDING

Bonding securely is the very cornerstone of a person's life. Some kind of bond affected us even before we were born. A woman's attitude about being pregnant, her state of mind and emotions, and her physical and emotional health all contribute to the cornerstone. Babies already "know" something of their world before they leave that warm and snug environment inside. The first hours and days outside the womb are vital to his health and well-being, setting the foundation upon which he will grow. All of us continue to bond one way or another throughout life.

A secure bond is the foundational bond that each person needs in order to be healthy in all respects. Bonding takes place in the brain within what we called the Attachment Center (Level 1) when we looked at the emotional side of the brain in Chapter Three. But all bonds that people build are not secure bonds. According to Dr. Daniel Siegel and other researchers, there are four styles of bonds, only one of which is a secure bond. Secure bonds are based on love. The other three are based on fear. As we look closer at these types of bonds, I will describe them using Dr. Wilder's interpretation of Chapter Three in Dr. Siegel's book, *The Developing Mind.* Dr. Wilder has "renamed" three of the attachment styles so that they are easier to remember. As we look at them, we will again see why synchronizing is so important to good development. We shall call the four types of bonds (1) Secure, (2) Dismissive, (3) Distracted, and (4) Disorganized.

As you read through the information on the four bonds, here are some questions to consider and answer:

Which of the four bonds do I think I had as a child?

What kinds of bonds have I seen modeled around me?

How do I want to bond differently with my own children?

Do I know a person who bonds/relates well who might mentor me?

What strengths for bonding do I have?

What weaknesses do I bring to bonding with others?

Where might I need to seek help or repair for existing bonds?

What do I turn to for comfort?

Keep these questions and your answers handy as you read. We will look at them again.

SECURE

A secure bond is one that is based on love and desire and is not based on fear. Bonding begins at birth, at first by smell, even before the infant can see. Keeping the infant warm and giving him or her food adds to positive early bonding. At about the sixth week touch helps the bonding process. When the infant can see better around three to twelve weeks, he begins to interact more and build joy. Around twelve weeks bonding continues with voice tone and facial expressions. In a secure bond, the parent synchronizes with the baby and watches closely how the baby is feeling, matching the baby's timing, intensity and tone as they interact building joy and quiet. Through the bonding process, by three months of age, baby has a picture in his mind of what his mother feels about him. We want that picture to be framed in joy.

During a joy-filled bonding process, the parents are attentive to the baby's needs for comfort, food, and protection, meeting those needs in a timely manner. A secure bond is built with lots of cuddling and holding. The baby feels safe and loved. He or she does not encounter angry faces or negative voice tones. The atmosphere around her may be calm or filled with "happy noise," but in either case, fear and anger are not part of her world.

Baby is not looking for fear. He is looking for someone who is glad to be with him—the definition of joy. As the new brain technology evolved that enabled researchers to observe the living brain, scans of what we are calling the Attachment Center (Level 1) of the brain showed an actual "light" that comes on in the brain when a person wants to bond or draw close to another. This desire is communicated by the brain in non-verbal communication—through eyes, through sounds, through body movements. Baby looks for a face and eyes that will sparkle with joy at seeing him. He is looking for joyful faces. When he wants to disconnect he will look away and up towards the left.

This little light is the key to bonding and how it progresses. In a secure bond the light goes off and on according to the desire of the child to be engaged with another. A good parent knows when to engage (draw close) and disengage (back off), following the pattern of the child. A secure bond is about the baby and his desire, not about the parent. This is synchronization, when mother follows the baby's need for attachment or quiet and both of their attachments lights go off and on together. Baby learns that connecting is "good." (p. 39 *Living With Men*) This attachment light works the same way all of our lives and thus we can again see the importance of synchronizing with others.

Another aspect of knowing, at any age, that connecting and relating is a good thing comes from each person in the relationship having the freedom to "come and go." Being free to come and go is the basis of a good bond and it starts with early synchronization. In such a relationship neither person clinches, controls or holds on to the other in any way that would hinder the other's growth and uniqueness. In infancy and childhood, we symbolically express this freedom to "come and go" in the dance of synchronization where the caretaker stays aware of the child's need to connect (build joy and bond) and disconnect to rest. Children are not actually free to come and go from the home at a young age, but synchronization is an emotional interaction that will later become an actual physical event. As a child grows into greater maturity the *symbol* of freedom will remain as we allow a teenager to try his or her unique wings at the same time he or she is coming and going *physically* from the home.

When adults are in a joy-filled relationship, freedom to "come and go" fosters an authentic, healthy relationship where one person does not try to control the other person by telling them what to do, think, feel and become. One person does not punish the other for having desires and interests that may be different than the other's desires and interests. Being free to "come and go" without fear of retribution is part of synchronization and one sign of a secure bond, whether coming and going is symbolic in the early years or actual in adulthood. Vanessa from Chapter Two has a secure bond. Like Vanessa, adults with a secure bond thrive, are relational and a joy to be around. If you are in a relationship that does not allow you to "come and go," talk to someone about it.

DISMISSIVE

In a dismissive bond the baby's/person's little "light" in the Attachment Center (Level 1) stays off most of the time because his need for closeness has gone unnoticed or been dismissed through rejection. Unlike the secure bond, which is based on love, this bond is based on fear, as are the other two at which we will look. When baby's emotional needs go unmet, or are not synchronized with well, the child fears that no one will dependably synchronize with him, so he "gives up." The parent ignores the child's desire to connect by being rejecting or emotionally unavailable and eventually the child pretends that this is all right. (A child can portray a false self as early as eighteen months of age.) Kaleb from Chapter Two had this kind of bond.

Nothing will ever hurt more than having one's attachment light ignored. (Wilder) The pain from being dismissed and ignored will cause a child to decide that wanting to connect is "bad" and he or she will try to hide the need for it. Since the child is "pretending" that all is well, in the family there may be an appearance that the child is a very good child, when in truth, he resigned himself to not having his needs met when they arise. The damage from this type of bond may not show until it is time to bond with his/her spouse and children. (p. 40 *Living With Men*) What we want to look at in this study is what kind of bond we had and how is the bond we formed in early childhood affecting our relating today. We ask ourselves questions such as, "Am I dismissive to those around me? Do I pretend to be all right? Have I given up that someone will connect with me? Because a dismissive bond is about the parent and his or her needs, not about the child, adults with a dismissive bond find it difficult to connect with others and may appear independent, unemotional and aloof.

In order to avoid forming a dismissive bond, a baby's needs must be met immediately and joyfully up to about the twelfth month. Doing so builds hope. Around the twelfth month, as we will look at later, things change, but a crying infant needs attention and we must do all we can to figure out how to help. There are on the market right now a few parenting books that teach parents the dismissive type of parenting. They advocate letting a newborn cry himself to sleep in the crib whenever the parent decides it is time. The infant eats when the mother decides. Everything is scheduled firmly by the parent, even at a very young age. Babies do need a schedule, but not too early. They eventually come to one on their own around three to four months but should never be left to cry it out early in the first year. Some of these books speak against "attachment theories" but after we understand how God designed the brain, we cannot agree with such a form of parenting. As adults, we want to avoid carrying over the practice of rigidity, controlling and selfishness that only considers our own needs and not the needs of those with whom we are in relationships. Being ignored is very painful.

DISTRACTED

Like the dismissive bond, the distracted bond is also based on fear instead of love. Again because of inconsistent synchronizing, in a distracted bond, the child fears he might miss getting his needs met because they get met so sporadically. His little "light" stays on all the time. This child is needy and clingy and gets very upset when caregivers are out of sight. Daniel in Chapter Two had a distracted bond. The distracted bond is also about the parent instead of about the child. Because of her own neediness, the mother wants the baby to synchronize with her. She looks for the baby to meet her needs for closeness when *her* "light" is on, regardless of the baby's desire at the moment. (p. 40 *Living With Men*) A mother distracted by her own neediness, with intrusions of unresolved issues from her past, often approaches the baby for closeness when she needs it. Not being in tune with the child's state of mind, and ignoring the baby's desire and signals for closeness or quiet, her interruption will distract him and then he will cling to her. Sometimes a needy mother gets pregnant thinking that having a baby to love her will bring her happiness.

Adults who have a distracted bond will seem to have emotions that are too intense and will often seem needy and clingy. If as an adult, we realize that we seem to latch on to others and want them to meet our needs, it is time to get some help for the painful wounds inside. God is the only one who can meet our deep needs, though we do loving things for each other. A distracted bond makes a big hole in one's heart that can cause relationship problems with others from whom we are trying to get life. Neediness attracts unhealthy responses.

DISORGANIZED

The most harmful type of bond is a disorganized bond, when the attachment light comes on and the desire to draw close produces unpredictable or scary reactions from those around the baby/person. Fear is the cement in all parts of a disorganized bond no matter what the age. The person is trying or wanting to bond with either someone who is angry at him, someone he fears, or the one with which he wants to bond is afraid of someone else. This leaves a baby with no one who can soothe him, as the caretakers are caught up in their own unresolved pain. This is the kind of bond that Jessica in Chapter Two had. No one can thrive in this kind of fear-filled environment. All of us desire closeness based on joy, on someone being glad to be with us. When desiring closeness brings anger, fear or too much intensity, a person becomes disorganized. He will have difficulty coping and it will be very difficult to relate to others. When babies grow up in an environment filled with anger and fear, it sets the stage for future mental illness and poor relationships. (p. 41 *Living With Men*) Disorganized attachments from a life filled with fear and anger are very painful. The problems in later years caused by such pain are numerous, ranging from people who are deeply fear-based to psychopaths who harm others.

Disorganized attachments can happen all through our lives, even if that is not the kind of home in which we grew up. They occur any time we want to be close to someone we fear, usually because of anger. Anger that causes fear is destructive and harmful. Maturity level, unresolved wounds, triggers, and joy capacity determine how a person handles anger. We have to address uncontrolled anger and get help for its underlying causes. There is no place in joy-filled relationships for abusive anger, sarcasm and other forms of verbal abuse. We must get help to eliminate these from our lives and homes.

Abusive or uncontrolled anger *physically damages the brain* of the recipient. It is physical, not just mental or emotional. It makes a "spot" on the brain that can be triggered throughout life. It is associated with the *disorganized bond* that we just talked about, when a person wants to get close to (or bond with) someone of whom they are afraid. Wrong expressions of anger bring fear into any relationship and the relationship cannot function correctly. When one of the "spots" on the brain gets triggered, Dr. Wilder calls this dysfunctional condition a **Disorganized Attachment moment (DA)**. The following information about DA moments is from conversations I had with Dr. Wilder.

I began to understand **DA moments** first hand from Dr. Wilder when I understood I had experienced one. It was not a pleasant lesson. A DA moment is a given moment or situation when we are afraid of someone with whom we want or need to get close. The fear can be for many reasons—fear of rejection, fear of disapproval, fear of more anger, fear of disappointment, or fear of humiliation.

Because few people recognize this brain malfunction, there is little training about it. No one wants to experience it or even talk about it. A DA moment is very painful. As we look around and observe or hear others talking about the fear they have with someone with whom they want to get close, we will see that DA moments are everywhere.

The desire or need to connect with someone takes place in the Attachment Center (Level 1), but when fear is present in that desire or need to connect, it causes Attachment Pain. You will remember that Attachment Pain is the worst kind of pain we can feel. Fear prevents the connection, causes Attachment Pain, harms the relationship and/or moves the person towards an addiction to medicate the pain.

The fear involved in DA moments can have levels of intensity varying from mild to extreme. Mild DA moments are common and easier to face. Here are a couple of examples of a mild DA moment: 1) You have to tell your pastor that you can no longer serve on a committee. You feel afraid and maybe worried about what he will think of you, but it is most likely mild enough that you will plow through the fear and talk to him. 2) Your mother is coming for a visit, and you are afraid that she might disagree with something you do with your child while she is there. You have a low level of dread about the coming visit. In both examples, you want to connect or draw close, but fear is involved.

Although many fear-based interactions can be mild, when the conditions are right, a disagreement or misunderstanding can quickly escalate to a Disorganized Attachment moment with extra-high levels of fear and anger, triggered because of the "spot" programmed into our brains by the abusive anger and sarcasm we have received in the past. When the body temperature changes during these emotions, (and the spot is there) the brain will heat up, and not only will the Relational Circuits go off, but chemical changes also will make the brain operate differently than it does when we are not highly angry or afraid. The Relational Circuits will shut off, but the meltdown will be more intense and the techniques we are accustomed to using for repair don't work. It is like operating a computer where you are working on Microsoft Word and it suddenly changes to Star Office. It would do no good to continue trying to work with Word. You would just get garbage. In the midst of a DA moment we try to act like we would if still in our regular ways of relating (Word), but nothing we are used to doing works the same in the DA moment (Star). Not being able to repair the relationship brings more pain and frustration.

An intense DA moment is much more difficult and painful to experience with the person who originally caused the "spot" with their anger and fear towards us. It will take a lot of work with outside help to avoid these "spots" getting triggered if we are still in a relationship with that person. Not wanting to cause such a brain "spot" should be a big motivation for parents to avoid uncontrolled and abusive anger, so that these kinds of triggers will not get programmed into a child's brain. We do not even want to think about what happens to a child that lives constantly in this kind of anger-filled environment.

As humans we were not designed to be in this DA state of mind. We hate it and are supposed to hate it. It is unnatural and is a result of

© 2012 Barbara Moon

the Fall of Man--a brain malfunction. We cannot work things out by usual methods nor make it work by trying harder. It's not designed to work because it is not natural—we are freaked out and the brain is momentarily fried.

Understanding that nothing we are used to doing will work at that moment will help us to stop analyzing the problem and get some help from someone who is objective. The more we understand how DA moments work and how they don't work, and the more we realize the potential for conflict they carry, the better we will be able to avoid them. *Not fearing ruptures or conflict* will help us avoid a DA moment. They feed on fear. Believing we can face the fear involved with wanting to connect and draw close, along with skills for *returning to joy,* are the keys to working out of a DA moment.

When the Disorganized Attachment gets triggered in the Attachment Center, we cannot willfully un-foul the circuit nor expect *usual methods* of calming to work. This moment of intense anger and fear is very powerful. We do not *have* to follow through the emotions and do the action that is connected to the trigger, but the pull to do so will be very strong. This powerful emotional pull needs the greater power of the Holy Spirit to bring us through the fear and anger to joy and peace. Reliance on the Holy Spirit and getting objective help are the paths out of a DA moment cycle if one gets triggered. Hopefully as one or both seek help to return to calm, the relationship will become a better one. (Wilder)

Because unhealthy anger can be so destructive, I have come up with what I call *Eight Commandments for Everyone*, though of course the list is not all inclusive.

EIGHT COMMANDMENTS FOR EVERYONE

Please don't bully

Please don't call names

Please don't use too much sarcasm

Please don't use put downs

Please don't yell or curse

Please don't threaten

Please don't ignore anyone's "no."

Please don't withdraw your love & shut others out

Maybe looking at how abusive anger affects the brain will motivate us to learn a better way and take the necessary steps to change harmful behavior.

Now that you have looked more closely at each of the bonds, let's review the questions, along with your answers, that you considered at the beginning of this section:

Which of the four bonds do I think I had as a child?

What kinds of bonds have I seen modeled around me?

Do I know a person who relates well who might mentor me?

How do I want to bond differently with my own children?

What strengths for bonding do I have?

What weaknesses do I bring to bonding with my child?

Where might I need to seek help or repair for existing bonds?

What do I turn to for comfort?

If after looking at your answers, you feel hopeless and messed up, here's what you might want to consider. The basis of professional counseling is exploring one's childhood. Depending on your need, a Christ-centered counselor could be a great help. As I said in the maturity chapter, small groups at church, conferences, regular church attendance, and being mentored all help us to grow. The very fact that you are reading a book on relationships says that you want to grow, so don't be shy to ask for help.

SYNCHRONIZING JOY—THE FIRST YEAR

We have just looked at the importance of bonding and how tuning in to a newborn's needs and meeting them timely are important aspects of secure bonding. We have seen how important synchronizing joy and quiet is in helping people feel loved and wanted. People thrive and bond best with whoever brings them joy. Love (secure) bonds grow through shared joy and those strong joyful bonds help minimize stress as joy keeps our brains functioning the way God designed them. I believe that joy and what it means is important enough for a closer look. Again, we will be looking at both the ideal and how it applies to us as adults.

Joy means that someone is glad to be with me—no matter what. They are glad to be with me at whatever level of maturity I am and my emotions do not frighten them away. Joy means that I am the sparkle in someone's eye and they light up when they see me. We are creatures of joy by our Creator's design; it's our natural state. (Wilder) The Scriptures are full of verses about joy. Joy seems to be extremely important to God. In one concordance, I counted over 160 verses just with the word "joy." Here are a few examples:

Joy and Strength: Do not be grieved, for the joy of the Lord is your strength. (Nehemiah 8:10)

Fullness of Joy: In Thy presence is fullness of joy. (Psalm 16:11)

Joy is the Youngest Emotion: For when the sound of your greeting reached my ears, the baby leaped in my womb for joy. (Luke 1:44)

Joy Gave Jesus His Strength: . . . who for the joy set before Him, endured the cross. (Hebrews 12: 2)

Joy is Why Jesus Spoke to Us: These things have I spoken unto you. . . that your joy may be made full. (John 15:11)

Joy Brings Us Through Trials: Consider it all joy, my brethren, when you encounter various trials. (James 1:2)

Why Jesus Said We Should Pray: . . . ask and you will receive that your joy may be made full. (John 16:24)

Joy is Why Scripture Was Written: And these things we write that your joy may be made complete. (1 John 1:4)

Joy is Why We Fellowship: . . . I hope to come to you and speak face to face, that your joy may be made full. (2 John 1:12)

We Are Each Other's Joy: For you are our glory and joy. (1 Thessalonians 2:20)

Joy Characterizes Disciples: And the disciples were continually filled with joy and with the Holy Spirit. (Acts 13:52)

Joy comes from Godly parenting: And he who has a wise son will joy in him. (Proverbs 23:24).

I have no greater joy than to hear of my children walking in the truth. (3 John 4)

Joy and Health: A joyful heart is good medicine. (Proverbs 17:22) [Building joy in the early months physically sets the foundation of the immune system. (Wilder)]

Joy is principally learned by *non-verbal* communication. As we saw earlier, the Joy Center (Level 4) is on the right side of the brain and communicates without words. Educators have long realized the importance of non-verbal exercises that can aid learning. When I was a high school Spanish teacher, I used marching, clapping, rapping, and throwing balls to help my students learn. In the same way, we build joy without words. Joy smiles are the best way. True joy smiles come from the Mother Core (Level 3), the third center we looked at in the brain's emotional control center. Cheesy camera smiles are not true joy smiles. Joy smiles light up the eyes and communicate to the other person that we are glad to be with them. Our eyes sparkle.

Kori's eyes sparkle with joy

Ryan in medium joy

Singing is another great joy builder and aids learning as well. Poetry and rhymes build joy, as do proper touching and pleasant smells. Though words are not the best joy builders, voice tone plays a very significant part. High voice tones communicate joy and approval. Low tones indicate disapproval. Matching energy (synchronizing) also communicates that someone is the sparkle in our eyes. Playing with babies or pets and enjoying elderly people can fill us with joy. Any activity that encourages us to be glad to be together helps fill the Joy Buckets of all involved.

Joy is what develops the brain, and keeps it running, as God designed it. Dr. Wilder uses an analogy of camping to describe the building of joy capacity. Joy Camp is our natural state, our destination each night (Ephesians 4:26) and where we want others to be with us.

We set up Joy Camp at birth by the bonding methods mentioned earlier—smell, food, temperature, tone, and later eyes and faces. Joy Camp is where we feel safe, loved and have our needs met. We want the newborn baby to know Joy Camp as the *normal state* of being, the "destination" which he will seek and return to the rest of his life. We want the same for ourselves and those with whom we have relationships.

Joy Camp is on top of a tall mountain. Babies have to practice climbing that mountain all the time. The more they practice, the higher they can climb. The higher they can climb, the more capacity for joy they will have in their Joy Buckets (the Joy Center of the brain) to help them cope with distress. We want the Joy Bucket to be both large (capacity) and also full. I will say more about this later.

For this writing we are going to assume that the mother is the principle caretaker, the person who takes baby up Joy Mountain by smiling, cooing and interacting face to face. Others of course can build joy with baby any time the baby desires. When the brain reaches its peak of joy building during the ninth month, baby will want to build joy up to *eight hours a day*. This makes it very important that mother is with the baby and that she is filled with joy herself. If mother is gone most of that ninth month, baby will be cheated out of some of his capacity growth.

SYNCHRONIZING QUIET TOGETHER

Another aspect of building joy capacity in the brain is synchronizing quiet along with the joy. For this book we are defining synchronization as "matching energy levels and being on the same wave-length or same page as another." We have used Dr. Wilder's analogy of good music—timing, intensity and tone. We saw earlier that a good mother is to teach her baby how to synchronize his brain and how to synchronize with other people. The mother accomplishes this, as we said, by communicating with her infant right brain to right brain, via left eye to left eye, at a rate of six times per second back and forth. This rate of interchange is below the conscious level and is totally *non-verbal* communication. Joy is built as the mother and infant interact with smiles face to face, break away for rest, and re-connect. When the mother stays in tune with the baby's needs to either climb Joy Mountain or rest, they are synchronizing joy and quiet.

As the baby's joy intensity rises, the mother watches for the baby to reach his or her highest peak of joy. The baby will then look away to rest. The difference in a good and bad mother happens here. If the bond is about the baby, the good mother will allow her baby to rest, lower her heart rate, and wait on the baby to coast down in intensity before building the joy again. A bad mother will not allow the baby to rest, but will continue to stimulate the baby past what he is able to handle—until he cries. She may continue pressing the child to smile in order to look good to others. She may subconsciously try to get the baby to meet her needs for closeness. When a mother takes her baby beyond his or her capacity level of joy, the baby goes into overwhelm. Over time this contributes to problems associated with the three negative attachment styles we looked at earlier, paving a path for problems down the road. Synchronizing quiet together is just as vital as synchronizing joy. Dr. Allen Schore's studies indicate that too much stimulation is even more harmful than too little. (p. 19 *Living With Men*) Alternating joy and quiet allows the baby to learn to synchronize his own mind as well as his relationships. The baby learns to be energetic, to be able to calm himself, and to build emotional capacity. As he rests after reaching the top of Joy Mountain, he learns that he can return to joy and eventually, with practice, he will be able to regulate his own emotions. (p. 20 *Living With Men*) We will look closely at returning to joy in Chapter Five.

Quiet together is not the same as being left alone. Quiet together means the baby knows someone is there with him even though the arousal state is a resting one. Not allowing a baby to rest after his or her peak of joy is reached is the main predictor of future mental illness. (Schore via Wilder) Again, this kind of interaction is about the adult's needs, not the baby's.

I don't know how many times growing up I saw an adult tickle a child until he or she cried or begged for mercy, forcing the child beyond his or her capacity into an overwhelmed state. This kind of harmful play is an example of de-synchronization. It should not be allowed. Healthy development is about both joy and quiet together. Joyful squeals of pleasure are part of building joy, climbing high up Joy Mountain, but it is up to the adult as the older brain to synchronize with the younger brain, and watch for that needed break to rest.

You may have memories of being pushed into overwhelm, or even pushing others past their limit. Learn how to synchronize both joy and rest by practicing the exercises in the Appendix. If you struggle with being able to quiet yourself inside, there are brain re-training exercises for that. If you do not have very much joy capacity, practice building joy with someone who does. It is never too late to build joy and keep your Joy Bucket full by interacting with others who are glad to be with you.

Greg and Kayli enjoy quiet together

SUMMARY

Secure bonds are based on love and desire—people synchronize. Dismissive, Distracted and Disorganized bonds are built on fear. People do not synchronize. Disorganized bonds are full of fear and anger. Abusive anger physically harms the brain, causing a "spot" that can be easily triggered. We can experience Disorganized Attachment moments of various intensities when we fear someone with whom we want to be close. High intensity anger and fear will cause a DA moment that is very difficult to repair. We need dependence on the Holy Spirit and help from a calm person to repair. It is imperative that we incorporate the Eight Commandments into our lives and replace them with joy.

Joy is the only emotion that infants seek on their own. Babies arrive already hardwired by God to look for eyes that sparkle and light up upon seeing them. Infants use body language, sounds and eyes to seek for that light in someone's eyes. If babies arrive from Heaven looking for joy, what could be more important than having parents who are filled with joy that will spill over into the baby's heart? What could be more important than being an adult who brings joy to others around us? Because God has made us creatures of joy, being glad to be with others (joy) is what we want for the basis for our relationships so that we can better handle the ups and downs of life. Climbing Joy Mountain develops emotional strength and capacity and a strong self. Allowing rest prevents future mental illness. Having joy and quiet capacity sustains us through life's sufferings, mistakes, disappointments and losses. What others see on our faces, reflecting to them how we see them, can determine how they see themselves. Will they see someone who is glad to be with them, or will they see anger and fear? Will we help them pack lots of joy up that mountain and allow them to rest or will we overwhelm them? Will we be strong under distress or weak and easily defeated?

The amount of joy we have in our Joy Center (Level 4) will greatly determine the answers to these questions about how we will live life and handle its disappointments and losses. When we synchronize joy and quiet, connection and aloneness, intensity and calm, while consistently validating and comforting distress, we will be bringers of joy who thrive and grow love (secure) bonds with others around us.

Deep satisfaction comes from sharing and building joy. God designed us for joy to be the basis of making it through hard times. As we give and receive life, everyone's emotional life grows to maturity and we will be more likely to reach our God given potential.

CHAPTER FIVE: RETURNING TO JOY

Goal: to understand the Big Six Emotions and how to return to joy.

INTRODUCTION

This chapter is very important for maintaining joy-filled relationships. Returning to joy is another way of describing part of what takes place when we seek and grant forgiveness, but there is more to it when looking at how the brain functions. The ideal age for learning to return to joy from negative emotions is twelve to eighteen months, God's window for building the circuits in the brain. From 2000 to 2010 I lived with my son, Greg, his wife, Chris, and their four girls—Tyler, Kayli, Kori and Brenna. During the early years, the girls were just the right ages for learning the brain skills that I was studying. As the twins, Kayli and Kori, hit the "return to joy" age from twelve to eighteen months, we observed and noted when they were in the Big Six emotions as we helped them learn to return to joy from those emotions. We were able to get pictures that illustrate these very events. I trust that the pictures and definitions will help you understand this important relationship skill.

As we go through the chapter, we will again look at the ideal that God has designed for building return-to-joy circuits. Many of us did not receive the ideal training; therefore, at the same time we look at the ideal, we want to continue looking at how the material applies to us as adults and where we need remedial brain training. It will be helpful to notice which emotions are those from which you do not know how to get back to joy easily. The ideal age for learning to return to joy begins around the first birthday and continues through the second year.

TWELVE TO EIGHTEEN MONTHS

Around a child's first birthday, a good mother who has a well-trained Mother Core (Level 3) will intuitively know it is time to start upsetting her baby. Up until now we have done very little to upset baby, being careful to meet all needs as they arose. We were delighted to synchronize joy and quiet and practice climbing Joy Mountain together. Now mother and baby will work on returning to joy from negative emotions, because about this time the baby becomes mobile and all is no longer sweetness and smiles. This period of time is very important as parents lovingly guide baby into and back out of these negative feelings so the brain can form "back to joy" circuits. (Wilder)

The way Mother and baby have practiced climbing Joy Mountain during the first year, building greater and greater capacity for joy, will determine the capacity of the Joy Bucket. The size and fullness of the Joy Bucket will then determine how well the baby can regulate his emotions and handle distress. Joy strength determines the capacity to persevere during intense moments

Kori (age 1) is ready to work on return to joy

During this crucial two years, it is important that the mother and other close caretakers have their own Joy Buckets running over. It is vital that mother and daddy have support from each other and others in their community; that they have life giving experiences, so that their Joy Buckets will be full enough to fill the baby's Joy Bucket and help him or her build return-to-joy circuits in the brain. At any age, we can only learn return-to-joy skills in relationships that function in joy. As we saw earlier, we can only "download" what we already have; therefore, as we go through the study, it will be helpful to note the negative emotions with which we struggle.

DEFINING RETURN TO JOY

There are six basic negative emotions common to all cultures from which all of us must learn a path back to joy in order to have the best relationships. The six negative emotions are disgust, sad, fear, shame,

© 2012 Barbara Moon

anger and hopeless. Joy is the seventh basic emotion. (Siegel). Dr Wilder defines "return to joy" as "reconnecting with someone who made me feel distressed." I have added to this definition "being glad to be with someone during distress and helping them stabilize and calm." Not only do we want to reconnect with someone who has distressed us, we want to have the capacity to be glad to be with others who are distressed and need help. You may remember in Chapter Two with the thriving chart, under *THRIVING*, that "return to joy" was part of Level 3. When I was growing up we called it "making up." Our goal in good relationships is to be able to stay together when emotions get intense, and when we know how to return to joy, it is much easier to avoid a meltdown. We do not fear conflict with people with whom we know we can return to joy easily.

When we know how to return to joy, the brain stays synchronized and we maintain our maturity and ability to hear another person. We are better able to discuss what is bothering us and come to a solution. With paths back to joy built into our brains, these Big Six emotions are not as scary and dreaded.

So let's look at how the path building takes place when parents are working on return-to-joy skills. For the return-to-joy circuit to get built successfully for a negative emotion, two things have to happen: the parent must share the bad feeling with the child (synchronize) and then return to joy (be glad to be together in the feeling and reconnect.) The child's brain copies the parent's brain as the parent shows the child how to feel the feeling, quiet the feeling and stay relational and flexible at the same time. (p. 23 *Living With Men*) When the parent (or bigger brain) synchronizes the bad feeling and stays glad to be together during the feeling, this experience makes a return-to-joy path that is stored in the Right Hemisphere of the brain. What I did in the van with the girls and the bee, and with the twins and the bear mask, is an example of returning to joy from fear. How the bigger brain handles the emotion is key, regardless of the age of the person they are trying to help. When doing remedial re-training with adults, there are brain training exercises that help build the return-to-joy circuits. You can see these in the Appendix.

When experiencing the negative emotions, the capacity strength for climbing back to joy from one of the negative emotions will be directly related to the earlier strength developed climbing Joy Mountain with Mommy in the first year. When the path is there and joy strength is adequate, return to joy takes under ninety seconds. (Wilder)

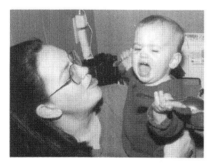 

Chris-and Kayli who's angry.   *Returned to joy in ten seconds.*

As an adult thinking about negative emotions, ninety seconds may sound strange to you. And when we look at the definitions of the emotions, they may not fit with your understanding about these feelings. It is helpful to note when thinking about returning to joy in less than ninety seconds and seeing the definitions of the emotions that babies' emotions are going to be mild in comparison to how we as

© 2012 Barbara Moon

adults view the emotions. Remember that the age for the baby to feel the emotions and build the path back to joy from the emotions is twelve to eighteen months. These are foundational, right-brain circuits and under normal conditions, the baby will grow capacity and practice them over a long period before having to feel them more intensely as we do when older. If babies do have to feel these negative emotions too intensely, we would call that a trauma.

Before we look more at building these paths back to joy in the brain, let's look at the definitions of the basic six emotions that will help us better understand them. The definitions are taken from notes I've made at Dr. Wilder's conference on thriving:

THE BIG SIX EMOTIONS

Disgust: *"Something here is not giving me life."* The word *life* in this definition refers to all kinds of life, not just physical life. Something doesn't fit here; something is not supposed to be like this. When Kayli and Kori, my twin granddaughters were around eighteen months, among many other crazy things they did were some disgusting ones. One day I caught the two of them in the bathroom. They had taken toilet paper and dipped and sloshed it up and down in the toilet, splashing water all over the floor, the seat and themselves. At the moment I arrived and opened the door, with my trusty camera in hand, I snapped a picture of Kori with the wet toilet paper in her mouth. Wet toilet paper in the mouth is definitely an example of something that does not give life to either the participant or the observer.

Kayli and Kori -- Disgusting Fun

Also around the time the twins were this age, I cannot tell you the exact number of times that Greg, Chris or I had to wash babies, cribs and walls after their naps. You guessed it—poopy on everything. I estimate it to be over thirty times. In spite of us pinning and taping them into "straightjacket pj's" they did it so often that they learned to say, "No poopy da wall." Besides lots of practice making that path back to joy from disgust, those events contained lots of returning to joy from shame as well.

Shame is such a misunderstood and difficult emotion to deal with that it demands an entire book. At this writing, *Facing Narcissism in Ourselves and Others*, a book about shame and its complexities is in process. I am helping Dr. Wilder write this book from one of his CD's, *Munchie 24*. In Chapter Seven we will revisit shame and see how narcissism develops from a lack of return-to-joy from shame. For now, we will continue looking at the emotions from the infant viewpoint and the ideal for learning the path back to joy from shame. But it is my experience that very few of us have this path, and that lack seems to be one that causes many, many relational problems.

Shame: *"I'm not bringing you joy and you are not glad to be with me here."* We can "not be glad to be with baby" when she does or brings us something disgusting, but shame can also arise any time someone is not glad to see us, or we are not glad to be with them, because of how we, or they, are acting. The definition here is extremely important because we are not talking about what I call "toxic" shame that denigrates and calls a person "bad." "I'm bad" is the most common way we think of shame and the most common way many have been given shame messages, thus making shame hard to deal with. God designed our brains in such a way that shame, or as Dr. Wilder calls it, "anti joy," is a signal that something needs correcting, something is off track. Someone is not glad to be with me because my behavior is off. It needs correcting. This is the whole basis for God's discipline of us, and our correction of each other. When we know how to return to joy from shame, it is not such a bad emotion. If we do not know how to get back to being glad to be together, defending, accusing, blaming and retaliating abound. Growing a path back to joy from shame is one of the most neglected and misunderstood paths of all the Big Six.

When someone is "not glad to be with me" and I have no path back to joy from that feeling, it can be very painful. Ideally over time, countless moments of not being glad to be together, but staying together with loving discipline and helping return to joy will build that path in a child's brain.

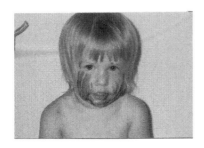 

Brenna -- A Self Portrait -- Shame　　*Kori -- Busted – Shame*

Here is a catchy way to think about shame: "I'm not glad to be with you right now (shame), but I will be glad to be with you (joy) while I'm not glad to be with you, so we can share the distress of what you have done, correct your behavior and return to joy."

The goal of working on shame is to be able to be glad to be together again. There are times where behavior is not acceptable and the child/person should feel shame. Without a path back to joy from shame, getting a message that someone is not glad to be with them will cause a person to become defensive. Defensiveness, and redirecting the "shame message" back on the sender, is a good sign there is no strong path back from shame. If the other person also gets defensive, it could be a sign that neither has a good path back to joy from shame.

Fatigue or low joy may be a factor when having difficulties with a shame message, but consider the need to work on how you handle shame when you encounter defensiveness in another or yourself. Learn not to fear telling your child or others that you are not glad to be with them here because something is hindering your joy of being close. We will expound on shame in Chapter Seven.

Sad: *"Something important to me is lost; I lost some of my life."* Babies, adults and children of all ages feel sad when they lose something. It can be something small or large, tangible or intangible, seeming important or unimportant to others. When someone is sad, we need to synchronize with their feelings, validate the feelings and give comfort that fits their need. If we want to build or strengthen a path back to joy from sad, we do not try to "fix" the person. We just sit with them and synchronize with them. We share the sadness while being glad to be together (joy).

Connor Got a "No" – Sad

Many people do not know what to do with disappointment and getting a "no" from someone, part of losing something important. Men have been taught not to cry or show sadness. Most women go to sad much easier. Knowing how to return to joy from sad, having someone to validate and comfort the feelings, will build and strengthen return-to-joy circuits in the brain.

Fear: *"I want to 'get away.' Something bad is about to happen."*
Below are pictures of one-year old Tyler, scared of a new experience. We placed her in a pile of leaves in order to take a pretty autumn picture. She was frightened. Mommy sat down beside her to synchronize and bring her back to joy from fear.

Chris and Tyler -- Fear   *Mommy reassures Tyler -- Fear*

In the third picture, after Mommy got down beside her and assured her (non-verbally) that it was safe, she liked the leaves. Tyler is returning to joy, but because the right and left hemisphere of a baby's brain do not connect until the age of three, you can see joy on one side of her face and fear on the other. The camera caught her face in the middle of the change.

Chris with Tyler, halfway back to joy

Anger: *"I need to protect myself and make it stop; I'm about to lose something important.to me."* Anger rises when we are about to lose something that we don't want to lose. It may not even be ours to have, but we don't want to lose it. Again this something we are about to lose could be tangible or intangible.

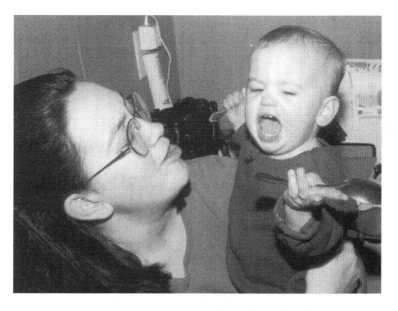

Kayli wants to keep the spoons – Anger

We want our children to be able to express anger in healthy ways. We do not want them to stuff or repress it: therefore, it's very important to help the little ones work on this path back to joy. In the bonding section we have already looked briefly at what happens when we live in an atmosphere filled with anger. We will look some more at anger in Chapter Ten.

Hopeless: *"I lack the time, capacity and/or resources to solve this. I'll never get back to joy."* Dr. Wilder points out that hopeless despair, like shame, can be one of the most difficult emotions to feel and re-train as adults. Few people are willing to share this emotion and help the other person return to joy. It takes maturity. In order to help others learn to deal with hopelessness, we have to have the path back ourselves. We cannot download what we do not have. A path back from hopeless can be learned with a good mentor, but of course it will take time.

Kori is devastated -- Hopeless

As we already said, it helps to keep in mind that the level of hopelessness a baby is feeling is not deep depression as an adult might think of the word, but rather the feeling of not being able to get needed help. For adults, the way we are defining it here, it is when we realize it would be wise to "give up" and wait for guidance or help, because we see that the resources to handle the situation are not available right now.

From these working definitions of the Big Six, we can quickly see that returning to joy does not necessarily mean being happy, with everything fine and dandy. Joy means I am glad to be with you no matter the situation and I want to be with you so we can reconnect even if I am the one who distressed you--or I don't *feel* like being with you. We want to stay relational and get back to calm. God upsets us quite often, but He is always glad to be with us and share in the upset.

Let's take a look at the necessary ingredients for learning to return to joy, defined as "reconnecting with someone who upset me," and/or "being glad to be together in distress."

In order to learn to return to joy, someone **HAS** to be glad to be with us **DURING** each the six emotions. The following are the basic components of returning to joy:

Share the distress

Be glad to be together

Stay relational

Use kind and comforting voice tone and touch

Help regulate emotions

Model how we act like ourselves

Have quiet together.

As you consider this list, let me share a true story that happened to one of my best friends, Debbie, and her family. The Sellmann's story will illustrate what returning to joy is all about.

Scott, Debbie, Rebecca, and Andy

A RETURN TO JOY STORY

One night long ago, a wonderful family of four heard a huge storm over their neighborhood. Scott, Debbie, Andy and Becca listened as lightning flashed and thunder, mixed with blowing rain, crashed around their house. The thunder boomed, but the loudest roars were from the wind. A tornado was coming to their very street.

Quickly Scott and Debbie gathered their young children and rushed to the basement for safety. But they soon realized that the basement was not safe enough. They were going to have to take their children through a low door into a crawl space up under the house where Scott stored the lawn mower. It was full of cobwebs and the floor was nothing but dirt.

By now the children were whimpering with fear, but Daddy and Mommy assured them they would be together no matter what. After entering the crawl space, the parents huddled with a child in each of their laps. They were so glad to be together while this scary storm blew all around them.

Mommy began to sing softly to the children. While the storm raged above they comforted one another. The noise grew to crescendo as a tree crashed through their roof into the kitchen above. While all around their house the tornado tore up other trees, broke windows, stripped the neighborhood of roofs and scattered debris for miles, the precious family sat quietly together under the house.

Daddy prayed, Mommy sang and the children snuggled in their laps as they waited for the terrible, noisy storm to pass. Hours later the stillness outside echoed the quietness of the little family's creepy refuge and they crawled back to the opening to stare in amazement at the damage around them.

# # # #

After reading the story, as you refer to the list of components for returning to joy, ask yourself these questions: Did the Sellmann parents do each of these components? Were they glad to be together in the middle of a distressing situation? Was this returning to joy about happiness and being fine and dandy? It took some time for happiness to return, but joy (glad to be together) was there right in the middle of the situation.

When in a distressing situation, the synchronization that takes place between the person with the "older" brain who can remain calm and the younger brain that is distressed allows the younger brain to mimic the older brain. This happens through the non-verbal communication we have already discussed. The younger one learns what it is like to "act like myself in this type of situation." He gets internal answers to the question, "How is it like me and 'my people' to act in this kind of distress?"

Let's review what it means to "act like myself." Dr. Wilder says, "I am acting like myself when what I am doing matches who I am, when my actions reflect my heart, even during intense emotions." Children learn to go to joy/peace or fear in a situation by watching and downloading what the parents do during intense emotions. This is done rather subconsciously as they read the parents face, body language and other non-verbal cues. During the distress, joy (or lack of it) will determine if a person has the strength to "suffer well," thus passing on peace (or more fear) to others around them.

Jesus is our best example of acting like oneself and suffering well during intense emotions. In Mark 3: 1-5 we read a story about Jesus being angry. This is not the story about turning the tables over in the Temple. That story does not give us an emotion word in the Greek; it simply states that Jesus did it. In the Mark story we have the Greek word for "rage"—*ogre*. As Jesus enters the synagogue He sees a man with a withered hand. The people were watching Him to see if He would heal on the Sabbath, which was against their laws. Jesus called the man to come to Him.

In verse 5 we find the Greek word for rage: "And after looking around at them with *anger*, grieved at their hardness of heart, He said to the man, 'Stretch out your hand.' And he stretched it out, and his hand was restored." Although Jesus was in a powerful rage, what did He do? He healed the man. If he had been at a picnic, what would He have done? He would have healed the man. If he had been teaching the multitudes, what would have happened? He would have healed the man. Jesus acted like Himself because His actions matched who He is and reflected His heart. It is like Him to heal, no matter which intense emotions He might be feeling. (Wilder, THRIVE Conference)

Our components of returning to joy contain another phrase that might need reviewing. What does it mean to "stay relational" under intense emotions? Again, Jesus is our best example. He both acted like Himself and stayed relational while He was on the Cross. No person has suffered more than He did on that day. But while feeling intense suffering, He talked to John and Mary. He sang Psalms and talked to His Heavenly Father. He forgave the people who were killing Him and shared hope with one of the thieves hanging beside Him. Staying relational means I do not withdraw, shut down, panic, lose it, or attack someone when emotions are intense. I might *feel like* or *wish* I could do one of these actions, but I do not follow through with the feeling. I stay relational, act like myself and suffer well.

IMPORTANCE OF BACK TO JOY CIRCUITS

Our look at returning to joy brings us to some important questions: why is it so important to have the return to joy circuits in the brain? What happens when a person does not have the path back to joy in his brain from one of the Big Six emotions? The answer to these questions is vital to our growth and maturity and how we relate to others, to God and ourselves. If we do not have a path back to joy from any of these negative emotions, we will avoid the emotional pain that comes with that particular feeling instead of returning to joy in ninety seconds or less. When we avoid pain several problems arise, as the pain remains unresolved, festering inside us and causing many relational issues. Avoiding pain is a huge problem in our world as a result of the breakdown of the family—and misconceptions of pain.

Pain is supposed to mean "comfort is on the way." When we grow up with validation and comfort and staying connected during distress, we do not fear pain. I find few people who know that pain means comfort is on the way because they did not receive comfort as a child when they needed it. Realizing that pain and comfort ought to go together is life-changing, because avoiding pain is the opposite of suffering well. When we don't suffer well, we stop acting like ourselves, we stop being relational, and we lose synchronization and connection. These relational problems from habitually avoiding pain are difficult to overcome and prevent us from maturing and reaching our full potential.

Return-to-joy circuits are important for another reason. When a child does not learn to return to joy from negative emotions and thus avoids pain, it is very likely that child will head down a path to addictions. When avoidance is a normal response to pain, addictions develop.

Addictions are anything that brings pleasure (a high) in order to avoid pain or anything that helps us dull or medicate pain (a low). The addiction controls us to the point that we cannot stop it even when there are negative consequences. When a child has not received what is necessary for thriving (love, comfort, validation, and reconnection) or has been abused, the child will have obvious or underlying pain throughout his emotional existence. Because he does not know how to face and feel the pain and return to joy, he will turn to things that bring pleasure, such as alcohol, drugs, sex, masturbation, food, unhealthy relationships, spending or gambling. It does not take long for these pleasure-seeking activities to become an addiction that medicates the pain that the person does not even know he is hiding. In Chapters Seven and Nine we will look further at addictions and how the brain science re-training can help those who suffer from addictions.

Sidetracking is another reason that return-to-joy is important. If a child does not learn to return to joy from one or more of the six emotions, avoidance of that emotion causes sidetracking to another easier emotion. For example, we saw that a common emotion that is difficult to deal with is shame. If one does not have a return-to-joy path from shame, he or she will often sidetrack to anger. Going to anger is common in men. Women tend to avoid anger by sidetracking to sad and crying. Building return-to-joy paths in the brain prevents children from becoming "people pleasers" or "people haters," because they know how to repair ruptures and thus do not fear the emotions involved in conflicts.

When we know that returning to joy is possible and likely after a problem, it takes the sting out of having that problem. Repair (return to joy), not prevention of ruptures (disconnections), is the key in a relationship. (Wilder) All relationships will have conflict and ruptures. Ruptures and repairs are messy, but understanding that repair, not prevention of ruptures, is the key to relationships diminishes the burden of performing perfectly and keeps us from dreading ruptures and trying to keep peace at all costs. We don't have to go into a rage or withdraw when we hit a bump with someone because we know that we can and will return to joy—if we both take the time and effort to work through the conflict.　Again we can look at the life of Jesus for the best example of how life works. Hebrews 12:2 tells us that "for the joy set before Him, He endured the cross." Though Jesus endured more than anyone else ever has, ultimately being separated from His Father, He knew that They would return to joy.

Building return-to-joy circuits between twelve and eighteen months brings an added bonus that I leave here from the parenting book to encourage anyone who has relationships with children. These return-to-joy circuits minimize the intensity of tantrums.　Around sixteen months an "amplifier" turns on in the brain that intensifies the Big Six emotions—instead of anger we get rage and instead of fear we get terror and night terrors. If the baby's brain has return-to-joy circuits, the amplification of these emotions is just a harder work out from which to get back to joy. If not, it causes suffering in the more intense moments.

(p. 26 *Living With Men*) Around the age of eighteen months, daddies play a huge role in helping babies learn to regulate emotions. Daddy's "I'm gonna get you" games train the brain to regulate fear and aggression as long as Daddy knows when to stop and allow rest throughout the high intensity of "I'm gonna get you." Any stimulation that leads to crying would be harmful.

EIGHTEEN TO TWENTY-FOUR MONTHS

As we continue our journey through the Infant Stage, we can see that during the second half of the second year, the baby puts together her basic identity with the material we have given her as we synchronized and interacted together. We want that identity to be a joyful one. Before putting together his or her joyful identity, babies handle each emotion separately, with each emotion having its own brain center. Around eighteen months, as they are practicing returning to joy, the "joyful identity" region (the Joy Center, Level 4) attempts to grow a circuit that connects these six emotion centers into a "ring." After this takes place, the baby can be the same person no matter what he is feeling. This joy ring will later allow him to act like himself regardless of intense emotions. (p. 26 *Living With Men*)

Without the training in joy in the preceding months building joy and return-to-joy, these centers will remain separated and there will be no joy ring. This will cause de-synchronization when negative emotions get triggered. When we encounter the lack of a joy ring in adults, we say that the person is moody and acts differently when angry or scared. An incomplete joy ring is an invitation to behavior problems, mood swings, inability to self-regulate emotions, and addictions. We have already looked at another result of an unconnected joy ring—sidetracking to a different emotion. (p. 27 *Living With Men*)

As we have looked at both the ideal and the application for adults, we can see the importance of building joy capacity and return-to-joy circuits. As creatures designed for joy, it is obvious that we need to build and maintain our joy strength as the foundation for emotional health for a lifetime. Because there is so much at stake in these important tasks, let's review the two ways we build joy strength:

Climbing Joy Mountain	Returning to Joy Camp
Voice tone	Paths back from Big Six
Facial Expressions	Sing our way back
Smells, food	Psalms
Touch	Touch-I'm with you, you're safe
Temperature	Share distress
Singing	Stay relational
Pets	Pets
Babies, elders	Be glad to be together
Giving life	Synchronizing

Building joy strength is easy and fun, but what about those of you who may have grown up without great joy training.   There is good news: **the Joy Bucket never stops growing!** So as you participate in the activities that build joy, you can spread joy smiles everywhere and build joy whenever you see a loved one's face. Watch for those whose eyes light up when they see you. Do things with people you love to be with, even if there is occasional rupture and repair. Startle people in the grocery store or Wal-Mart by smiling at them. Tell all the pregnant or new parents you know to build as much joy and quiet as possible the first two years, the years that the Designer designed as the best time. Make building joy part of your lifestyle. Practice the exercises in the Appendix.

WHAT HAPPENS IN DISTRESS

Building joy is fun and beneficial but let's review for a moment what happens when the brain de-synchronizes if the Joy Bucket is not full or there is no path back to joy. When the brain cannot handle the level of distress it encounters, the Logic Center (Level 5, the Left Hemisphere) shuts down and the person is operating from the Joy Center (Level 4) where there are no words, only non-verbal communication. A person with his or her Logic Center off-line cannot "hear" instructions, threats or lectures.

When a person goes into distress that overwhelms and de-synchronizes the brain, exploring, listening and thinking stop. The way to help the situation is to return him or her to joy first. Remember the list for return to joy tactics? Use them. Synchronize, share the distress, be glad to be together, stay calm and return to joy. Discuss instructions and words when the emotions are not out of control, during a non-stressful time, *before* a meltdown occurs or *wait until after* you have restored joy. Keep in mind that words and instructions do not work when the Left Brain is off. Words and instructions just frustrate. The number one priority is to return to joy first.

CONNECTING THE TWO HEMISPHERES

Around the age of three, the Left and Right Hemispheres develop a connection, making it possible for the verbal and feeling halves of an infant's identity to discover each other. Before they connect it is actually possible to see two emotions on the same face as we did a few pages back.

After passing the third birthday and growing this connection between the two hemispheres, a person can begin to feel feelings and think about them at the same time. If the Left Hemisphere (Level 5) shuts down from distress the brain will operate as if the connection is not there. When it is connected and running, we can talk about and reason with the person about what is going on even when upset. If the Logic Center shuts down the person will turn into a one-year old. A one year-old, regardless how old the body is, thinks only of what he is feeling, and words do not help. When the Left and Right Hemispheres have not connected, whether developmentally, or from neglect or mistreatment, the brain does not develop properly. (p. 30 *Living With Men*)

According to Dr. Wilder, operating without the Left Hemisphere up and running is similar to driving on a road where the bridge is out. If we try to talk to or control someone with words, without the connection of the two hemispheres, disaster lies ahead. Feelings are in control. Dr. Wilder says, speaking of the child before the age of three: "When it comes to maturity, sooner is not better. If you were exploring a road that was just being built and came to a river with a sign, 'Bridge to be built next year,' would you try to drive your family across the chasm?" (p. 30 *Living With Men*) In the same way, if a child or person is past three and for some reason the Left hemisphere is undeveloped or shut down, he will act like a one-year old. Words do not help anyone who is acting like a one-year old. The bridge is out. (p. 31 *Living With Men*)

When the brain is synchronized from Level 1 to Level 5 there is a bridge between words and feelings and we can now change what we think. What we think can help us to change our feelings and we can talk about what is going on. (p. 31 *Living With Men*) Talking about feelings and changing them is regulating emotions.

SUMMARY

We have looked at the ideal for the four-year journey of bonding, synchronizing, building joy and quiet, returning to joy and learning to regulate emotions. These skills are foundational for healthy, thriving relationships, and good health. When we realize we did not receive some of what we needed to build a joyful brain that can return to joy from all six emotions, we know that we have some work to do. It will be good to get with others who want to build joy and re-train their brains. Hopefully along the way we have gained some explanations that will help us better understand ourselves and others, making our relationships more enjoyable. In Chapter Twelve there is a list of the *Nineteen Relational Brain Skills* that are taught at the THRIVE conferences. Throughout the book we will cover the basics of the *neurotheology* brain science and these relational skills. Review the Nineteen Skills list periodically as you assess your own grasp of which skills you are good at and which you need to work on. I have added Scriptures and a short definition of each skill. You can find more about THRIVE conferences at www.thrivetoday.org.

SECTION II—GOING DEEPER

CHAPTER SIX: THE IMMANUEL PROCESS, RELATIONAL CIRCUITS AND TRIGGERING

Goal: to recognize when we are not relational because of unresolved trauma and grow in our ability to hear Jesus' voice and be able to go to Him for healing, encouragement and guidance.

INTRODUCTION

Because most of us did not receive all that we needed growing up nor did we learn all the tasks that were necessary for maturity, we often find ourselves stuck in emotional pain without God's peace or a sense of His presence. What we need is to be able to interact with God *at the same time* we are feeling upset. In order to do that, we must be able to stay relational. Dr. Wilder, Chris Coursey, Dr. Karl Lehman and Ed Khouri have developed the Immanuel Process as a path to healing that shows us how to stay relational enough to interact with Jesus and resolve unsettling emotions that come from unresolved traumatic memories. We want to learn to go to Jesus during the upsetting emotions, or as soon as possible afterwards. This chapter will be a brief summary of how to go to Him using the Immanuel Process. In other chapters we will look more closely at some of the components outlined here. The Immanuel Process is fairly simple and can be done as a counseling session, a personal devotion time or in a group. It can be used to heal a painful memory, to show us that something in the present is about the past, or to hear God's voice for encouragement or guidance in general. The information in this chapter is a condensation of the Share Immanuel booklet that can be ordered from www.thrivetoday.org[8]

---

[8] *Share Immanuel,* E. James Wilder & Chris M. Coursey, 2010 www.lifemodel.org, www.thrivetoday.org

Following are the basic steps/questions on which we will elaborate further. Credit for Relational Circuits information goes to Ed Khouri.

Make certain that your brain's Relational Circuits (RC's) are on. Relational Circuits are on when the brain is synchronized in all the levels. (See the section "Relational Circuits" below.)

1) Next, find Jesus in a past memory where you sensed He was with you--or do **appreciation.** (See below) If you are not able to perceive His presence, you can ask, "What keeps me from perceiving You are with me?"

2) Sit quietly and sense His presence while thinking about whatever is, or has been, upsetting you. It is also helpful to ask Jesus to take you to the time and place in the past that is connected to and causing the upset. You can do this in writing in a journal as well. When you perceive His presence, ask these questions, sitting quietly and listening after each:

3) Ask Jesus, "What do You want me to know about this (situation, feeling, problem)?"

Ask Jesus, "Where were You during this painful event?"

Ask Jesus, "What did I believe about myself at this time?"

Ask Jesus, "How do You see what I believed about myself?"

4) When finished, show appreciation for His work in your situation.

5) Share the story of how He healed the painful event.

The questions we have listed do not have to come in this order. Sometimes God peace comes as soon as we know where Jesus was in the painful event. We may not be able to resolve a painful memory by ourselves until we practice, but learning to go to Jesus in a good memory, or doing appreciation, will set us on the path to hearing Him more easily.

It is possible to increase our awareness of God by practicing the Immanuel Process. My friend, Debbie Sellmann, of the tornado story in Chapter Five, has been working on the Immanuel Lifestyle for a while now and she sent me the following observation she had with her husband, Scott:

> Scott & I were talking a couple of mornings ago about finding God in hard circumstances and Scott said, "Like *Where's Waldo* . . . he's in the picture all the time, but you have to look to find him." (*Where's Waldo?* is a children's book series.)

> So then I thought about some of the games I like to do -- word searches, pictures where you are given things to find that seem not to be there on first glance, but when you search, you can ultimately find them. To me, word searches are like when I am feeling emotions swirling inside and words come, but it seems like a jumble until I ask Jesus where He is--and then His words stand out.

Debbie and Scott see the value of turning to Immanuel and asking Him the questions above when problems and pain arise in their lives.

THE BRAIN'S PROCESSING PATHWAY

Before we look further at the components of the Immanuel Process, it will be helpful to talk first about how the brain processes painful events and what happens when a painful event is not processed as God designed the brain to work. According to Dr. Karl Lehman, one of the important contributors to the material we are studying, a painful experience that has not been fully processed is what we commonly call a trauma. In his book, *Outsmarting Yourself*, Dr. Lehman goes into great detail about the pain processing pathway in our brains through which experiences must be processed in order to avoid it becoming a trauma, or if stored in the brain as a trauma, what has to happen in order for the trauma to be healed. Here is a brief summary of the pain-processing pathway. We will use this information in other chapters as well. Dr. Lehman's material is used with permission.

> When we encounter pain, our brain-mind-spirit system always
> tries to process the painful experience. There is a very
> deliberate pathway that this pain processing attempt will
> follow, and there are specific processing tasks that we must
> complete as we travel along this pathway, such as maintaining
> an organized (secure) attachment, staying connected, staying
> relational, navigating the situation in a satisfying way, and
> correctly interpreting the meaning of the experience. When we
> are able to successfully complete this process, we get through
> the painful experience without being traumatized. . . . and
> when we are not able to complete the processing journey, the
> painful experience becomes a traumatic experience and the

memories for these traumatic experiences carry unresolved toxic content. [9]

If you look closely at the specific tasks Dr. Lehman lists, you will see that there are five of them and that they correspond to the five brain levels which we have already studied. Level 1—maintain a secure attachment; Level 2—stay connected, don't de-synchronize into fear; Level 3—stay relational; Level 4—go through the experience in a satisfying way (or go back to it and see what would be satisfying); Level 5—understand the meaning and how it fits into my life. Completing these tasks during a painful event prevents trauma being stored as a traumatic memory, and completing them in an Immanuel moment heals and removes the unresolved toxic content. What we need, either during a painful experience or afterwards to heal the painful experience, is a joy-filled relationship. None of the five tasks can be accomplished without another person present. That person can be Jesus, Immanuel; God with us.

God is always with us, even when we do not perceive His presence. (Matthew 29:20, Hebrews 13:5, Luke 24: 31-32). God wants us to actively remember the times we are aware of Him. (Deuteronomy 8:18, Psalm 105:5, Mark 8:18) As we saw above, we begin the Immanuel Process by going to a memory of a time when we *did* perceive God's presence. If we are not able to go to a place that we did perceive His presence, we can think of anything that we appreciate. **Appreciation** is anything that makes us go, "Ahhhh." (See the section "Appreciation"

---

[9] Dr. Karl Lehman, *Outsmarting Yourself*, This JOY! Books, 1117 S. Milwaukee Ave., Suite A4, Libertyville, IL 60048 pp. 329-330 www.kclehman.com

below.) The beach, a sunset, the mountains, a baby sleeping, a campfire, a warm blanket—any of these are things that make us feel peaceful and they are all from God whether we recognize it or not. Remembering a previous interactive memory or doing appreciation are both ways to take us to a place where we can begin the Immanuel Process.

RELATIONAL CIRCUITS

Beginning the Immanuel Process with our **Relational Circuits (RC's)** on is vital.[10] As Dr. Wilder, Ed Khouri and Dr. Lehman tell us, if the RC's are not on, we cannot relate to anyone, including Jesus. You will remember from Chapter Two that the brain has to stay synchronized in order to function as God designed it. If we do not have enough joy built up in the Joy Center of the brain, or we get triggered, the brain will de-synchronize and we will not be able to process the painful memory. When the brain is de-synchronized we are not relational. The Relational Circuits are off.

When we are in a non-relational mode with our Relational Circuits off, we are not acting like our true selves because the defenses are up. Defense mechanisms include anger, toxic shame, accusing, blaming, controlling, withdrawing and attacking. When these attitudes or actions are going on, we cannot relate because we are either defending or withdrawing. It is useless to try to solve a relational problem when the brain is melted down and non-relational.

[10] Relational Circuit information is from *Belonging Facilitator Workbook*, Ed Khouri, E. James Wilder, Shepherd's House Inc. P.O. Box 40096, Pasadena, CA 91114 pp. 48-49

GETTING THE RELATIONAL CIRCUITS ON

Before beginning the Immanuel Process, or any other time the RC's are off, whether alone, helping another person or in a group, we can do one of three physical exercises to assure that the RC's are on. In his *Belonging Workbook*, Ed Khouri has named this process *Shalom for My Body*. [11]

Tapping

In the center of the chest, the vagus nerve (it runs parallel down the center of the body) is closest to the surface of our skin. By tapping back and forth with each hand (fingers) about the speed of the heartbeat and taking a deep breath, we can reset the brain and bring the RC's back on and calm the brain. After tapping the chest, rub softly with the fingers and at the same time say the verse, "Whenever I am afraid, (upset, angry, etc) I will trust in You, O Lord." (Psalm 56:3) Repeat a couple of times. This exercise is the easiest and can be done driving down the highway with one hand back and forth or done obscurely when needed while around other people.

Startle Reflex

---

[11] *Belonging Facilitator Workbook*, Ed Khouri, E. James Wilder, Shepherd's House Inc. P.O. Box 40096, Pasadena, CA 91114 page 59

We have all seen newborn babies do the startle reflex. For resetting the RC's, we throw our head and arms up and back, taking a deep breath. As we lower our arms, we say the verse, "Whenever I am afraid, I will trust in You, O Lord." Repeat two more times.

Yawning

For this calming, re-synchronizing exercise, we take a deep breath like a yawn, turning the head first to the left and then back to the center, saying the verse. Then yawn to the right, return to the center and say the verse. Repeat. It is not necessary for it to be a real yawn.

Appreciation

Thinking of something that we appreciate will also reset the RC's. Dr. Wilder recommends having at least three appreciation memories we can go to when upset. After you think of something that makes you feel like saying, "Ahhh," give the memory a one-word name, such as, "beach," "campfire," or "flowers." If you share your appreciation memory with someone, tell them the name and then if they are with you when you de-synchronize and your RC's go off, they can help you get them back on by saying the name. (See Appendix Exercises for Chapter Six)

THE PROCESS

Now that we have our RC's on, we want to take a moment to find a memory where we knew that Jesus was with us and we perceived His presence. It can be any time, even our salvation experience. As we perceive His presence (or we have done appreciation instead), we simply talk to Him about what is going on and begin to ask the questions we listed above such as, "What do You want me to know about this?" As we listen, we trust that what we hear in our minds is He, unless what we hear does not fit with His character. (We will look more at how to distinguish God's voice in Chapter Nine.) If there seems to be a blockage of some kind such as a "wall," a "curtain," or "blackness," we ask Jesus, "What do You want me to know about this blockage? What do You want me to know about why I can't hear You?" In fact, whenever we have any blockage, painful event or memory, we ask Jesus, "What do you want me to know about this?" We do not ask "why" questions. If we ask "why" questions, we will almost never get answers. Did you just ask why? (p. 9, *Share Immanuel* booklet)

In addition to asking Jesus what He wants us to know; we can also ask Him to take us back to the place and time in which the painful event happened. The painful event could have just happened, been an hour ago, a month ago, or years ago. As we go back to the place the memory began, we ask Jesus, "Where were You when this happened." The answer to this question is the main point of the Immanuel Process—that when an event was not processed through the brain levels because we were alone and had no validation and comfort, we did not think about, realize, or remember that Jesus was there. Dr. Wilder states in the *Share Immanuel* booklet:

Whether we are thinking about a painful event or the memories of those painful events are triggered accidentally, we feel the upset that is still actively hiding God's presence and peace from us. Since our memories are incomplete because they do not include God's response to us in the pain memory, the pain is still there. The event has not yet become a source of wisdom and reassurance of God's presence in our lives. (*Share Immanuel*, Page 3)

When Jesus shows us where He was in a painful event, it changes everything. We no longer feel alone; we no longer feel the intensity of the pain of what happened; the unresolved toxic content of the memory is no longer easily triggered. Jesus has healed the memory and set us free. Freedom from painful wounds makes it easier to relate to those around us. We do not need questions such as, "Who started this?" "Whose fault is it?" and "Who needs to change?" The trigger is healed.

WHAT IS A TRIGGER?

So what happens when a painful memory has not been healed and resolved? What do we mean by "trigger and triggered?" Again we can turn to Dr. Lehman for a good explanation:

A trigger is any stimulus in the present that activates memory content. A trigger can activate both traumatic and non-traumatic memories. . . Most people use the word for traumatic memories With respect to psychological trauma, we are triggered when something in the present causes our brains/minds to open traumatic memories so that unresolved content from these memories is activated....Various unprocessed aspects of the experiences, such as unprocessed physical sensations, unresolved negative emotions,...and distorted interpretations come forward and *feel true in the present.* (p. 331 *Outsmarting Yourself,* paraphrased.)

Understanding how a trigger makes pain from the past feel true in the present is another life-changing principle. When toxic content of a memory is not resolved through the brains processing pathway, everyday events can trigger the pain associated with that memory. More often than not, our RC's go off. Conflict gets worse and finding solutions feels hopeless. Unless we know there are two types of memory we have no idea the pain is from a trigger. *Explicit memory* is what we normally think of as memory—"Yesterday I _____." *Implicit memory* does not include the feeling that I am remembering something from my past and it affects me without being noticed by the conscious mind. (Lehman) Many relationship problems are the result of triggered, unresolved painful memories.

THE VERBAL LOGICAL EXPLAINER

There is a part of the brain that contributes to the problems we encounter when triggered by unresolved pain from our past. Dr. Lehman has named that part of the brain, in the Left Hemisphere, the Verbal Logical Explainer, or VLE. This VLE helps us make sense of the world and is constantly giving us explanations of what is going on around us. That is not a problem as long as the explanations are based on what is true.

The VLE is not malicious, but it can only give us an explanation based on the data it has. If that data is distorted by an unresolved trauma in our lives, the explanation will be much distorted. This is especially upsetting when that unresolved trauma gets triggered by someone in front of us. The result, if we do not recognize that the VLE's explanation is based on a trigger, will be that we believe the VLE when it tells us that *the person in front of us is the problem.* We will lose all the benefits of having our RC's on, we will blame them for our upset and we will not want to find a solution other than one that requires them to change. We all have experienced this. (Lehman)

Dr. Lehman tells a story about him and his wife that illustrates his triggering and the VLE's explanation. This scenario happened nearly every time they prepared to leave for vacation.

Because of an unresolved incident from his childhood, Karl was driven to extremes when ready to leave for vacation. He liked to leave for vacation at 6:00 AM sharp. At 5:59 he would be in the car waiting on his wife. She was inside doing adult things such as setting the thermostat. When 6:00 arrived and they were not leaving, he would get very upset, becoming de-synchronized, losing his RC's -- and his maturity. His VLE would tell him that his wife was the reason for his upset. Among other explanations about her being the problem was, "If she had just gotten up earlier, everything would be fine."' Karl was upset with his wife, who had not done anything wrong, because he was triggered with the unresolved issue from his past. The trigger turned off his RC's and his anger increased as his VLE's explanation made his wife the problem. (pp. 30-31, *Outsmarting Yourself*)

As this brief story illustrates, it can be very hard to recognize when we are triggered because the pain we feel seems *real in the present* and seems to make sense that *the person in front of us is the problem.* The memory that is making the trigger is invisible, coming from the part of the brain that stores *implicit* memory. Dr. Lehman calls a distorted memory's false content an "invisible memory" or "Memorex" (not live.) The result is that we lose our peace and the ability to relate to anyone, *including the Lord*. Just as the VLE can give us wrong explanations about others, it can also tell us that God is the problem when we are triggered from past traumas. If we want to improve our relationship with Him, knowing how triggers and the VLE function can be a huge motivation for us to receive healing through the Immanuel Process.

As we look at receiving healing from triggers, it is important to note that traumas do not have to be huge to set up this commonly occurring dilemma. Any time a child is not validated, comforted and taken through the processing pathway of a painful situation, it will be a trauma. It does not have to be a fire or a tornado or abuse; it can be an everyday event, such as rejection on the playground, where the child was not able to handle the pain. When triggered in the present, the toxic pieces of the past event will come forward into the present. The toxic pieces coming forward and feeling true in the present distort our perceptions and emotions and we blame the person who triggered us.

So an important question arises. "How can we notice that we are triggered?"

I find the easiest way to tell that I am triggered is when whatever is going on in the present *FEELS MUCH BIGGER* than the situation calls for—it is way out of proportion. If that happens, and I can notice it, I will immediately do the chest tapping exercise to get my RC's back on. Sometimes I go to an appreciation moment to get calm. I might ask myself questions such as, "What does this remind me of from my past? What do I need here? How old do I feel?" Later I will go to the Immanuel Process and the Lord about it: "Lord Jesus, what do you want me to know about that upset?" "Is it coming from something in my past?" If I cannot work it out by myself with Him, I will ask someone to help me.

The other way to notice we are triggered is to learn to recognize that our RC's are off because we are irritable or intolerant. The THRIVE material lists these ways to know if our RC's are off:[12]

I want to make a problem, person or feeling go away.

I don't want to listen to what others feel or say.

My mind is locked onto something upsetting.

I don't' want to be connected to someone I usually like.

I just want to get away, fight or I freeze.

I more aggressively interrogate, judge or try to fix others.

"My goal is to perceive the Lord's presence, tell Him about my pain and receive His comfort so that I can get my Relational Circuits back on line." (RC's card from www.thrivetoday.org)

---

[12] *Belonging Facilitator Workbook*, Ed Khouri, E. James Wilder, Shepherd's House Inc. P.O. Box 40096, Pasadena, CA 91114 page 61

SUMMARY

God designed our brains with a pathway through which to process pain. When we were not validated and comforted during or after a painful event, it is stored as a trauma. Unresolved past traumas can be triggered and feel true in the present. The Verbal Logical Explainer will tell us that the person who triggered us is the problem. During a trigger, our brain is desynchronized and our Relational Circuits are off. We cannot relate to anyone, including the Lord. When our RC's are off, we lose our peace and feel upset; it does not feel good. We need to disengage and get calm by doing a *Shalom My Body* exercise before further interaction with anyone. We can say something like, "I'm triggered right now. I need some time to calm down." We turn to the Lord through the Immanuel Process to see what He wants us to know. The Immanuel Process brings healing of the old, unresolved traumas from the past that trigger us in the present. When Jesus comes into the painful memory and shows us where He was and how He saw it and gives us the validation and comfort we did not get in the past when it happened, everything changes. The trigger is gone! It no longer FEELS true that the other person is the problem. I again see them as my loved one.

As we get better at spotting triggers, noticing our Relational Circuits are off, and going to Jesus for healing, we will see our relationships increase in joy and grow deeper in intimacy.

CHAPTER SEVEN: REVISITING SHAME— THE REMEDY FOR NARCISSISM

Goal: to understand how narcissism develops as a result of no path back to joy from shame.

INTRODUCTION

In Chapter Five, we looked at the Big Six emotions: anger, fear, disgust, hopeless, sad, and shame. It seems that one of the most difficult of these emotions to feel, to return to joy from, and to understand is the emotion of shame, and for that reason, we want to revisit shame. When there is no path back to joy from shame, the way a person behaves when given a shame message causes huge relational problems. Psychologists call this type of problem *narcissism.* At this writing, I am helping Dr. Wilder write an entire book on the subject of shame and narcissism. *Facing Narcissism in Ourselves and Others* will take a close look at this difficult subject, beginning with the Scriptural basis and ending with application for how to handle ourselves and others when dealing with narcissism. Much of what we will look at here comes from Dr. Wilder's teaching on shame and narcissism.

WIRED FOR JOY AND SHAME

In Chapter Five we looked at shame in relation to how babies around the age of twelve to eighteen months learn to return to joy from shame. God has wired us humans to be creatures of joy. Joy means "someone is glad to be with me; I'm the sparkle in someone's eye." God has also wired us with circuits of *anti-joy*, commonly called "shame," and defined as "someone is not glad to be with me right now." God wired us with an anti-joy system for a very good reason. When we find out or realize that someone is not glad to be with us, it is meant to be a loud signal that we might have some behavior that needs attention and that behavior is keeping us from being close to someone we love. Good parents use this anti-joy system all the time when properly disciplining their children. Like the good parent He is, God intends for us to humbly "hang our head" in shame so that the behavior can be corrected. Feeling shame is not a bad thing, although many of us think it is. Let's look closer at the differences.

TOXIC SHAME

The shame that babies ideally learn to deal with is not destructive, nor is the intensity of shame that a young child feels in order to practice returning to joy the same as what most of think about when we discuss shame. Unfortunately, because it is a difficult emotion to deal with, most of us grow up without knowing how to return to joy from "good" shame, and as we get older, the destructive kind of shame grows inside our belief system. Destructive shame is what most people think of when they hear the word *shame*. I call it "toxic shame." Toxic shame hits us when we are told—or believe—that *we* are bad based on our behavior. Toxic shame messages attack our personhood instead of separating our behavior from our personhood. Separating personhood and behavior is a vital skill for joy-filled relating. For example the difference can be seen if saying, "You are a liar," versus, "You lied." Correcting the "bad" behavior with toxic shame communicates that *we* are bad. Since so many of us have been reared believing our acceptance and worth are based on our behavior instead of Christ, toxic shame is everywhere.

These old messages we have heard and believe from the past, along with little capacity for returning to joy, trigger toxic shame any time we hear correction or disagreement, even at times the message is not toxic. Fights break out, defense mechanisms take over, or punitive withdrawal abounds. The Relational Circuits are off. This greatly impacts relationships because we cannot relate to defense mechanisms (anger, blame, threats, control, accusations, and toxic shame)—we can only relate to other people. If we can get healing from the baggage of toxic shame and learn to return to joy from shame, then "good shame messages" will be less likely to set off disagreements. It takes maturity to operate this way, but learning to give good shame messages is worth the effort.

GOOD SHAME MESSAGES

A good shame message says something like this, "What you are doing is keeping me from wanting to be close to you and I would like to be close, so can we work this out?" Good shame messages are the opposite of toxic shame messages. A good shame message has the purpose of bringing us closer after we have looked at something that keeps us from being glad to be together. When we humbly consider a good shame message upon finding out that someone is not glad to be with us, God can work changes in us. But unfortunately many people do not humbly listen to loving shame messages, but instead get defensive and try to justify themselves. When we give shame messages to people who do not know how to return to joy from shame, they often are unable to receive even a good shame message. They refuse to listen; they attack; they redirect, turning the message back on the messenger. When rebuked or corrected, they cannot bear to hear any message that says they may have a problem.

STIFF-NECKED NARCISSISTS

In the Scriptures God has a lot to say about people who refuse to hear that they have a problem. He uses the Hebrew word *qasheh* (kaw-SHEH) over and over to describe people He calls "stiff-necked." We are calling them *narcissists*. Narcissists are people who refuse to hang their heads. *Qasheh* can also be translated as obstinate, rebellious, un-teachable, prideful, harsh, etc. Isaiah 8:4 and Exodus 32:9 are two examples.[13]

When we are in a relationship with a narcissist who acts *qasheh* and does not know what to do with a shame message, conflict will occur if there is any hint of correction or lack of being glad to be

---

[13]E. James Wilder, Ph.D., *Munchie* # 24 and future book, *Facing Narcissism in Ourselves and Others*, www.lifemodel.org

together. The most common response from the person who does not know how to get back to joy from shame and cannot take correction is to bully the one giving the shame message. Most often the narcissist will turn the message back on the person bringing the message in order to make sure that they do not feel any shame. Instead of hearing that we want to correct something in order to get close, the narcissist wants the messenger to feel the shame for them. Narcissists are masters of tracking others' failures so they can use them against other people. They know what they are doing and what will hurt others. The pain of being attacked or shut out will cause the messenger to back off and stop the "correction" or rebuke. What the narcissist is doing is bullying.

Bullies, even those on the playground, seem to come in two flavors—those who back down if someone stands up to them and those who escalate when someone calls their hand. We do not usually know which type we are dealing with so fear of what they might do keeps us from saying what needs to be said. "It won't do any good," and "but they will get angry," are the two most common fears that keep us from speaking to behaviors that prevent true, joy-filled connection. We end up apart and not really glad to be together when what we want is to be close. The narcissistic bully gets his/her way and does not have to humble himself/herself before God and others and feel "good" shame. The result is a lonely bully who leaves others rejected and wounded, while he or she misses the chance for a better life full of joy-filled relationships. The solution is to learn how to return to joy from shame, learn to humbly check with God about the messages we hear about our behavior, and learn to overcome fear of speaking when needed.

God has to free us from the fear of what response we might get when having to say that we are not glad to be with someone. It takes healing of our old wounds and old patterns, plus a clearer understanding of how God views stiff-necked people and to what He might call us to speak. It is not a small fear that hinders us from obeying God and speaking to someone who will not allow themselves to feel shame and bow humbly for correction. That fear of having their toxic shame turned back on us, being attacked in anger, or being made to feel another's feelings is a very strong fear. We have to learn what, when and how God wants us to give a good shame message, because what we all want with both God and others is to be close and to be glad to be together.[14]

There are numerous ways to look at narcissists who growl or attack others because they do not want us to communicate in any way that we are not glad to be with them. On the opposite side of responding to shame messages, there are people who do not growl or attack the messenger upon hearing a shame message, they attack and beat up on themselves. Dr. Wilder has descriptive names for both kinds of narcissists. He calls the growly bullies "Peacocks." He calls the quieter, self-attackers "Skunks."

> *Peacocks usually attack anyone who gives them a shame message. Skunks on the other hand, beat up on themselves. If they get a shame message, they will turn around and say, "Oh, I stink. I'm awful. No one loves me. I'm not worthy." They beat*

---

[14] In this section, let it be understood that there are some people who are not safe to be around. These paragraphs would not apply to dangerous relationships.

themselves to a pulp until the other person does the same thing he would have done with a peacock—tell them something on the order of, "Oh no, there's nothing wrong with you. I'm sorry I said that. I won't say it again." We take back everything we said to correct them because they went around beating themselves up. With either style of narcissist, the same goal has been accomplished— to stop the shame message of correction. Neither will tolerate shame.[15]

As we can see from this brief paragraph taken from the Dr. Wilder's *Munchie #24* and the new book, both kinds of people who are unable to take a good shame message are behaving as narcissists. Neither can hear the underlying goal of drawing close. Both want the problem to go away instead of focusing on the relationship. Neither knows how to return to joy from shame, a task we are supposed to learn around 12-18 months of age.

A NEW TRACK

What adult, narcissist bullies need is a new track in their brain for how to return to joy (being glad to be together). Dr. Wilder gives us one solution for restoring a narcissist:

Narcissists are eager to keep track of all the things that will make others feel shame, because later on this might prove useful to them. They will always listen to someone else's shame story because they are trying to find out what causes others to

[15] *Munchie #24* and future book *Facing Narcissism in Ourselves and Others*, E. James Wilder, www.lifemodel.org

feel shame so they can bring it up again and use it to hurt or control. To them, having an arsenal of shame about others is very powerful ammunition. But suppose in the middle of our shame story we throw in a little nugget of how we learned from that; how we learned to be the kind of person God meant us to be. By doing that, we can provide a road back, a path back to joy in their brain, for the narcissist.

The narcissist will actually learn from listening to our story if we will share with them the shame in our life and how God brought us back to joy from that. If their narcissism is of the iniquity version (defined in the book as "things we learned to do the wrong way when young"), *they learn there is a way back from shame, the place they got stuck to begin with.*

In childhood, narcissists stuck in their iniquity never learned the way back to being close; they do not know there is a way back, so when we tell them the story, they follow us back. It is as if they are saying, "Oh, whoa! How did you get back there? How is it we started over here with unhappy to be with me and you got back to being glad to be together? That's an amazing trip!" As they follow that trip back with you, the interesting thing about the brain is that it learns there is a different way to relate. This is what is necessary for people who have been raised in iniquity.[16]

Dr. Wilder's narrative describes what we call a 4+Story. In the Appendix, there are instructions and examples for telling 4+ Stories

---

[16] Future book, *Facing Narcissism in Ourselves and Others*, E. James Wilder and Barbara Moon, www.lifemodel.org

that will help you learn how to tell them. Relating to our study of the brain, narcissism is caused by Level 4 not functioning well. The person did not have a stable three-way bond structure with validation and comfort that taught them to see others' perspectives and understand "us," versus "me." Without a strong, joy-bond full of validation and comfort, we cannot learn to return to joy and mature. Traumas cause us to get stuck at the emotional age in which they took place. As we help people experience authentic, joy-filled relationships through synchronization, joy building and 4+Stories they can build a path back to joy.

SUMMARY

Shame is a misunderstood emotion and the lack of understanding causes many relational disruptions. Most people think of shame as what we are calling "toxic shame," or shame that communicates we are bad. Babies are supposed to learn to return to joy from shame between 12 and 18 months. When they have not learned a path back to joy, shame messages that say, "I am not glad to be with you right now," cause people to defend and justify themselves instead of listening to the underlying message of "I want us to work on this so we can be close." God has much to say in the Scriptures about people who refuse to hear that they have a problem and refuse to humbly bow their heads in order to change. We are calling them narcissists and they come in two personality styles: *Peacocks* who growl and turn the shame back on the messenger; *Skunks* who beat up on themselves. Our fear of how a narcissist will respond prevents us from giving the "good" shame messages that they need to hear. God has to heal and grow us out of that fear. We can help others grow a path back to joy by telling them stories of how God brought us back. Working on our narcissistic beliefs and behaviors will go a long way towards improving our relationships.

CHAPTER EIGHT: REVISITING THREE-WAY BONDS—VALIDATION AND COMFORT

Goal: to understand the importance of three-way bonds and validation and comfort in relationships.

INTRODUCTION

You will remember that we looked briefly at three-way bonds in Chapter Three. The best three-way bond is built by joy with Mother, Father and baby. There we saw that the three-way bond was part of properly developing The Joy Center, Level 4, in the brain and was also the path to overriding fear at Level 2. As a person with a bigger brain becomes the "third face" beside another person and what they fear, the younger brain tracks away from the fear back to peace. In this chapter we want to look further at how joyful, three-way bonds build, re-train, and/or help maintain a strong identity. Thanks go to Ed Khouri for most of this section, used with permission. See www.lifemodel.org for more information on Ed's material.

BENEFITS OF A THREE-WAY BOND

The brain is wired for three-way bonds upon which we grow our identity. God has designed the brain to work best with mother and father joyfully bonding with the baby. How the bonds are built determines how strong the child's identity will be. We looked at the basics for developing Level 4, the Joy Center, and how the earliest bond with mother grows this area of the brain. At about seven months of age baby can explore his or her relationship with father at the same time he is interacting with mother. (Khouri)[17]

With this addition of a "third face," now the baby can learn about "us." Baby learns mind sight, what the world looks like from someone else's viewpoint and what is going on in someone else's mind. Before the capacity to do the three-way bond, the baby's viewpoint is very self-centered. The baby shares best one-on-one and that is mostly with mother. As the three-way bond develops, so does the baby's viewpoint. This will serve him well when he is distressed. It will be easier to "act like himself during intense emotions" when he has grown up with a three-way joy bond. How the parents see the child will determine how he sees himself later on. If the faces and eyes with which he has bonded are full of joy and love, that is how the child will see himself and others. It will be easier to see that God sees him that way, also.

When children have a joyful three-way bond, at times when they are not with the parents their mind remembers the three-way bond. They remember that Mother and Daddy were glad to be with them. Their bond is secure. This helps the child endure stress and keep a strong relational identity in the Joy Center. When the brain stays synchronized the child does not melt down during distress. All these things will help the child in school and getting along with others. The identity will be strong.

---

[17] Ed Khouri's yet unpublished material.

© 2012 Barbara Moon

TWO INGREDIENTS

Ed Khouri tells us that there are two main ingredients needed in the building of the strong identity through a three-way joy bond—validation and comfort.[18]   Let's take a closer look at these two ingredients:

VALIDATION affirms the reality of the pain and the experience that a person is going through. It does not minimize or exaggerate the pain; it tells the truth. When we validate, we let the other person know we are aware of their experience and that they are important. Validation comes before and during comfort. It is sharing a mutual mind state with the other person, another way of saying we are synchronizing (see Chapters Three and Four). Although much of validation is non-verbal, words that validate sound something like, "I'm so sorry this happened to you. I will do whatever I can to help you." (Khouri)

COMFORT helps the person in pain to see what God sees. It's always relational and shows His truth and His heart towards us. During comfort, our mind sight is repaired as we see other perspectives. Comfort is done best non-verbally via voice tone and appropriate touch as we communicate something like, "I did not want this to happen to you; I will weep with you; I will help restore you." Comfort is not to be a

---

[18] *Belonging Facilitator Workbook*, Ed Khouri, E. James Wilder, Shepherd's House Inc. P.O. Box 40096, Pasadena, CA 91114 pp. 58-61

time of trying to fix the person. We sit with them in their pain. It is not the time for saying truth, quoting Scripture or admonishing. Return-to-joy comes before instructions. Comfort is the opposite of condemning, controlling and ignoring. We want people to learn that "pain means comfort is on the way," so that they will not fear and avoid pain. (Wilder.[19]) Finding comfort with others feels wonderful, but sometimes others are not available right when we need comfort. Jesus is always with us and we can turn to Him for validation and comfort any time. (2 Corinthians 1: 3-4) He told us He would help when bad things happen—validation. (John 16:33). He said He would never leave us or forsake us—comfort. (Hebrews 13:5-6) Comforting and validating ourselves also helps—if our Relational Circuits are on. Journaling is another good way to connect with Jesus or comfort ourselves. It is also good to *ask* a safe person for validation and comfort when needed.

If we ask for help and do not get the comfort and validation we needed from someone, it is helpful, after the crises, to help them see how they can better offer validation and comfort in the future. We want to do this calmly and kindly so as to help others learn and see the importance of learning that pain means comfort is on the way.

In summary, it is evident that a strong, joyful identity built from validation and comfort in a three-way bond is a plus in relationships

---

[19] Taught to me by Dr. Wilder in the 1990's. See *Jewels for my Journey*, pp. 86-88, Barbara Moon, www.lulu.com/barbaramoon, www.amazon.com or my blog on this topic- http://barbaramoon.wordpress.com/2010/08/24/pain-means-comfort-is-on-the-way/

where conflict and ruptures are certain to happen. An early, strong three-way bond increases the capacity to handle higher levels of distress, a huge factor in relational conflict and ruptures. Anything that helps us keep it together in distress will help us repair conflict.

WITHOUT A THREE-WAY BOND

Let's look at what happens when a person does not grow a three-way joy bond and does not receive validation and comfort. Whenever a painful event happens, without the three-way bond, a person has less capacity to endure the distress. When emotions are not validated, the person represses the pain and denies that something bad happened and after a while it will be difficult for them to show emotions.

Lack of comfort makes a person more fearful because they feel alone and uncared for. Without validation and comfort during or after a painful event, the person's identity waivers. As we looked at in Chapter Three, when the brain de-synchronizes, we cannot act like ourselves and stay relational. Lack of comfort and feeling alone are very non-relational.

If trauma occurs, the de-synchronization is worse. In the next two sections, though it is a bit technical, I want to share some information about how trauma affects de-synchronization, because some readers may need to hear it. Some readers may have experienced, or be experiencing, such extreme de-synchronizations—or be living with someone who has or does. We will look a little closer at how the emotional control center melts down under extreme overwhelm.

Trauma disrupts the control center and the brain begins to shut down from the top, Level 5, down to Level 2, where fear then runs the life. The *degree of disruption caused by pain* depends on a person's age, the severity of the pain, what their existing capacity is, and the attachments/bonds they have. Long-term relationships or a network of community can act like a safety net. Without the safety net, disruptions become more serious. (Khouri [20])

Most traumatic disruptions (including those from substance abuse) are below consciousness. An intense emotional swing without the ability to calm oneself shuts down the Left Hemisphere and the top levels of the emotional control center. The Left Hemisphere contains files, data, explanations, answers to "why" questions, and things we learned with words. When the meltdown occurs and the Right Hemisphere takes over, the left side fails and does not work. Access to all the information in Level 5 is lost. In the case of substance abuse relapse is profound. Most of the things the person needs to do such as lists of what to do, who to call, etc., are stored on the left side. One cannot get to the data of words. It is easy to see how this causes relational conflict and ruptures. (Khouri[21])

After losing the Left Hemisphere where words are stored, if a person loses Level 4 where memories are stored in pictures or images of what to do when distress comes, the melt-down will continue until Level 2 takes over and runs the brain until the stress or trauma is over. We have now lost our identity—what it is like us to do. Weak three-way

---

[20] From lectures by Ed Khouri and yet unpublished material
[21] From lectures by Ed Khouri and yet unpublished material

bonds with inadequate modeling of how to handle stress set us up to de-synchronize under painful conditions.

You will remember from Chapter Three what is lost when Level 4 goes off. We lose our access to personal identity, the ability to regulate emotions, joint focus, goal directed behavior, and moral and social behavior. We are unable to correctly interpret what is going on with others, we lose our maturity level, we are unable to act like ourselves and all of life is fear based. Our Relational Circuits are off.

When a person's identity collapses, their self-talk is distorted, they see God differently, and life and relationship are about "me," about surviving and about medicating pain. The person seeks validation and comfort from within the self, medicates pain, or seeks for others or things to fill the gap left by the pain of lack of identity. The things the person will rely on will be early attachments formed in the brain at Level 1—sex, codependency, alcohol, thrills, money, power, high grades, food. He or she will turn to whatever things or people that made them feel better or met their needs. (Khouri [22])

When the identity collapses and Level 2, which never shuts down, is running the brain, life is all about terror/fear or anger/rage. We see and treat people as objects. Logic, factual information and reasoning do not work. We do not think or act like a person.

---

[22] From lectures and/or unpublished material by Ed Khouri

DISSOCIATION

If extreme stress persists without validation or comfort, massive de-synchronization occurs. This is called "dissociation." Dissociation is an intense state of conserving energy by shutting down all but Level 2. Dissociation feels like "death" when the brain should have experienced quiet or calm. God designed the brain to experience high arousal (joy) followed by rest/calm. *When no rest comes after high arousal, it feels like death.* The person is feeling helpless and hopeless and desires to become "unseen" to conserve energy, foster survival, feign death to allow the mind to heal and restore depleted resources. When there is absence of a strong three-way bond, or intensity is too great it is very painful. All things are distorted about who I am. (Wilder, Khouri)

Once dissociation is used as an escape from overwhelming pain, it is hard to stop using it. It is a non-relational approach to coping. If dissociated, the person will not remember the trauma at all and will *fear and avoid rest*, because they experienced feeling "death" when they were supposed to feel rest. The use of dissociation as a coping mechanism is affected by the lack of validation and comfort during a trauma and the absence of an early three- way bond.[23]

If a person is used to dissociating and goes into treatment for substance abuse, he or she can do well in treatment, but because they compartmentalize, they can easily fall after they leave treatment. If the person has not had healing of the underlying traumas that cause dissociation and/or has not worked on re-training the missed brain

---

[23] If you have need of further study or understanding about dissociation, go to www.lifemodel.org These paragraphs are a brief look at a very complex disorder.

skills, leaving treatment will more likely result in failure because of triggering. (See Chapter Six about triggering) (Khouri[24])

Anytime unresolved traumas that are stored and un-remembered on the right side of the brain come forward, or get triggered, we will feel the feelings of the distress from that past unresolved trauma, but we will not remember that what we are feeling is from the past. The left side of the brain (the VLE from Chapter Six) will try to explain and make sense of what is going on. The VLE has no idea why we are feeling the way we are and it seldom looks past the end of our nose. It does not remember the trauma. The VLE will tell us it is about the trigger, most likely the person in front of us. The VLE is wrong most of the time.

The VLE can also give us an explanation about things that feel good such as addictions. The VLE tells us that this euphoria from something right in front of us, felt in the pleasure center (the nucleus accumbens), will help us again. It becomes a vicious cycle.[25]

BUILDING NEW THREE-WAY BONDS

Living is easier when we have strong, three-way family bonds which teach us there are other people in the world. We are better able to handle distress when not feeling alone. We can suffer well and not medicate our pain. If we had a strong three-way bond in the early years, we are a step ahead. If we did not, this is where a community

[24] From lectures or unpublished material by Ed Khouri
[25] VLE, triggering from Dr. Karl Lehman, *Outsmarting Yourself*, This JOY! Books, 1117 S. Milwaukee Ave., Suite A4, Libertyville, IL 60048 www.kclehman.com

with joy-filled relationships comes in. Family bonds bring strength to heal and grow and maintain stability. Since dysfunctional families are numerous, it is quite often within Spiritual family that we get help for validation and comfort needs. Spiritual communities based on joy help us heal and grow, practice joy and quiet, and create belonging. As we practice an Immanuel Lifestyle within a joy-filled community and tell the stories of our healings, others will find God's love and healing and the belonging which all of us need. (Khouri)[26]

A Spiritual community based on joy will help us find and enjoy joy-filled relationships, relationships that will strengthen the emotional control center, grow brain skills, and build strong three-way joy bonds. Through joy-filled relating we can build joy, do interactive quieting, breathe deeply together, and practice calming and quieting together. Others can help us know when our Relational Circuits are off and help us get them back on, which will, in turn, help us relate better and calm and quiet intense cravings. Experiencing belonging with others will help us connect with God and others in joy and returning to joy. In joy-filled relationships we will experience much needed validation and comfort and with Immanuel healing we can experience the presence of God in the bad places and/or just enjoy His presence. The joy will spread as we tell the stories of our healings and invite others to join us in growing deeper with God.

---

[26] From *Belonging Workbook* and/or other unpublished material by Ed Khouri.

SUMMARY

Joyful, three-way family bonds are necessary for developing a child's brain in the way that God has designed. These bonds insure a strong sense of identity, high capacity for stress, and a strong relational identity. Just as importantly, three-way bonds are vital for healthy relating throughout our lives. Experiencing a sense of belonging with others remedies lack of brain skills and promotes a sense of "us," helping us cling to God and others longer during distress because we are able to handle things together. A three-way bond gives us greater capacity to suffer well and not avoid or medicate pain that leads to addictions.

Validation of pain and comfort from pain prevent traumas, the collapse of our identities, and addictions. Lack of validation increases denial and lack of comfort increases fear, resulting in a shaky identity that can collapse more easily. If high stress persists, massive de-synchronization occurs, resulting in dissociation. (Khouri[27]) Traumatic memories are stored in the back of the brain, unresolved and subject to triggers that will bring them forth into the present, causing relational problems that are difficult to repair because the underlying pain feels true in the present. All of us need joy-filled relationships to help us fill in the places that our brains need re-training, the places we have not experienced a three-way bond, and the times we have not received validation and comfort. All of us need Immanuel healing that will become a lifestyle.

---

[27] Lectures or unpublished material by Ed Khouri

Thanks again to Ed Khouri for his information on three-way bonds and how they work. You can find additional resources at www.lifemodel.org Ed has full courses available for groups and churches that take people through extensive brain re-training and healing for addictions. Ed's material will soon be available with a new name and a new website.

CHAPTER NINE: SATAN'S THREE STRATEGIES

Goal: to recognize when we are avoiding pain, not living from the Spirit, and not hearing God

INTRODUCTION

Through the years I have found it very helpful to understand some tactics the enemy uses to trick and deceive us. In this chapter we will look at how Satan uses pain and the flesh *(sark)* to get us off track and how knowing the difference in God's voice and Satan's voice can keep us on track. First we will look at two strategies that Ed Khouri has developed in his *Thriving: Recover Your Life material*, a course for groups and churches, that combines THRIVE material and addiction recovery material. The first two strategies come from the *Restarting Workbook,* pages 43-44.[28]

THE FIRST TWO STRATEGIES

LIVING FROM OUR PAIN: The first strategy that Satan uses against us is to motivate us to live from our pain. This approach comes by living from the right side of our brain. Life is directed by feelings and/or avoiding pain. When a person is living from their pain, they

---

[28] [28] Ed Khouri, *Restarting*, Shepherd's House, Inc., Pasadena, CA, 2007, pages 43-45 www.lifemodel.org

relate to God and others by eliminating pain, hiding from pain, and using others to relieve or medicate pain—all attempts to avoid pain. Avoiding pain in these ways is the path to addictions. The enemy likes that trap.

LIVING FROM THE SARK: The second strategy Satan uses is to drive us to live from the *sark* (the flesh). Living from the *sark* is a left-brain approach. Life is directed by lies, wrong beliefs, trying to determine good and bad on our own. (Proverbs 3: 5-6) We try to pick the right or wrong course by what hurts or does not hurt and/or by what looks good or does not look good. We have a mistaken belief that we can pick a course of action that will not hurt. This is lie-based living. The *sark* is stubborn, persistent and always wrong. When living by the *sark*, we are looking at good and evil instead of looking at God. (Genesis 3)

Lie-based living is especially destructive when we experience trauma, because Satan will use not only the trauma to try to destroy us, he will use lies about the pain, lies about our perspective and lies about God to make it worse. As we looked at in Chapter Six, one of the needs we have for healing a trauma is that we can explain an event and fit it into our lives. If we are living by the *sark*, the explanations for life are based on the drive to eliminate, medicate or avoid pain. These explanations will be based on lies. We will not be able to fully process the trauma through all five levels of the brain. Satan will keep us defeated.

The enemy will not care if we know the Bible well if what we believe about God and pain is coming from the *sark*. A Biblically informed *sark* will cause its own problems. It is what crucified Jesus.

© 2012 Barbara Moon

Here is a brief summary of what we believe about pain when living by the *sark*:[29]

> The *sark* says: If it hurts or is bad it must not be God
>
> If it is less painful or good it must be God.
>
> If I serve God and it is painful, it must not be God's will, or I must be wrong, or no one cares.
>
> If I serve and it is not painful, it must be God's will. I'm right.

ADDICTIONS—THE RESULT

After looking at these first two strategies, it is easy to see how our relationships and lives can become dysfunctional if we are avoiding pain and/or living from the *sark*. The path of both these strategies is some form of avoiding pain. Living from pain or living from the *sark* diminishes our joy capacity and keeps us feeling separated from God. Living by the *sark* causes us to make choices based on lies that we think will keep us from pain. Avoiding pain is the pathway to addictions, one of the most difficult results of following Satan's strategies. Addictions are devastating to joy-filled relationships and are worthy of their own study, but here we will take just a brief look at how Ed Khouri sums up addictions.

Ed points out in the *Restarting Workbook* that if we live either from our pain or from the *sark*, the negative emotions we are avoiding will become wired to BEEPS. BEEPS are an acrostic for the following:

---

[29] Ed Khouri, *Restarting*, Shepherd's House, Inc., Pasadena, CA, 2007, Page 44

Behaviors (Work, activity, busyness, pornography, gambling)

Events (Thrill seeking, bungee jumping, sports)

Experiences (Sex, entertainment, TV, electronics, perfectionism)

People (Relationships, co-dependency, bonds based on fear)

Substances (Alcohol, drugs, food, sugar)

BEEPS are attachments to various kinds of addictions that we use to regulate emotions by increasing pleasure or decreasing pain. They help us artificially regulate emotions. Attachments to BEEPS take the place of our connection to God and others.[30]

Ed also points out how BEEPS become a cycle. We use BEEPS to regulate negative emotions and the negative emotions become wired to BEEPS. The negative emotions trigger BEEPS which drive us to use BEEPS. When triggered, it is almost impossible to avoid BEEPS. If our wiring is not changed, we will do the same thing over and over, expecting different results. We need God and joy-filled relationships to break this addiction cycle. People addicted to BEEPS need others with well-trained, joy-filled brains, who know how to handle the emotions and who are glad to be with them in their distress. (p. 45 *Restarting*)

Avoiding pain, living by the *sark* and battling addictions keep us from reaching God's potential for our lives and relationships. Knowing these destructive strategies, receiving healing from God and enjoying joy-filled relationships will free us from Satan's tricks to get us off track.

---

[30] Ed Khouri, *Restarting*, Shepherd's House, Inc., Pasadena, CA, 2007, pages 28, 44-45 www.thrivingrecovery.org

THE THIRD STRATEGY

FIRST PERSON SINGULAR: In the 1980's I heard another strategy that Satan uses to get us off track, and with no surprise, we find that this strategy also involves lies—lies that Satan disguises as *our* thoughts.

Many of us wonder if we are hearing God in our thoughts and we are afraid to trust what goes through our minds even when it sounds wonderful. Sometimes we trust thoughts that we should not trust—lies from the past, lies from Satan. These lying thoughts are like "old tapes" from our past that have always been part of our thought life. Dr. Bill Gillham and his wife Anabel, both now in Heaven with Jesus, taught that Satan can speak to us (in our minds) in "First Person Singular—I." When Satan speaks in first person singular, we believe it is our thought and thus take it as being true about us.[31] It is a very devious trick.

"I can't do anything right!" "I'm so stupid." "I always mess up." "Nobody wants to be with me." "I am alone." These are a just a few of those kinds of first person singular thoughts that the enemy uses to keep us in bondage and defeat. Satan's voice in our head correlates perfectly with events from our past, with just enough of "his truth" there to make us believe his lies.

Bill's idea about this tricky deception led me to come up with a list of ways to help us determine if the voice (our thoughts) we are hearing in our head is a lie from Satan or something from God. God sometimes

---

[31] Bill Gillham, Lifetime Guarantee, Harvest House Publishers, Eugene Oregon, 97402 1993, page 103. www.lifetime.org

speaks in first person singular, too. Often when considering our thoughts, the question arises, "What about *my* voice?" For this list, because I call it *Two Voices*, I put *our* thoughts on the side with God when they are thoughts that fit His character and/or how He sees us in Christ. If not, the thoughts go on Satan's side. Thinking of the choice as being only two voices makes it easier to determine, spot and reject Satan's lies. He does not want us to recognize when he is giving us thoughts that are lies.

Learning to distinguish these "two voices" helps us both reject Satan's lies and learn to hear God's voice more clearly. Satan's lies are thoughts that fit the *sark* (flesh) and/or the world while God's words fit His character and His Word. The more we practice believing that the thoughts we hear that are like God are from Him, the easier it becomes.

As we learn God's voice, it then becomes easier to speak conversationally, back and forth, and believe it is He because it would be like Him to say those things we are hearing in our mind. Interacting with God back and forth is the Immanuel Process we talked about in Chapter Six.

Now let's look at the list of *Two Voices*

SATAN'S VOICE:	GOD'S VOICE
Condemns	Convicts
Performance Based Acceptance	Accepts
Lies	Truth
Loud	Soft (1 Kings 19:11-12)
Selfish	Unconditional love
Discouraging	Encouraging
Worry, Doubts	Trust Me
Fear	Faith and Love
Presses Down	Lifts up
Death Giving	Life Giving
Dark	Light
Sin Conscious	Righteousness Conscious

Certainly there are other things we could come up with to distinguish the voices, but this list can get us started recognizing God and rejecting lies from the enemy. Here is an additional, brief part of a lesson from Anabel Gillham on how to "analyze the thoughts that invade our thinking processes:

A. This is a condemning thought.

B. This thought attacks my character.

C. This thought accuses me.

D. This thought confuses me.

E. This thought is designed to destroy me.

F. This thought is not true."

Anabel also recommends adding "In Jesus' name" to any thought to see if it fits with God's voice or the devil's.[32]

SUMMARY

The enemy is out to deceive and destroy us and he uses devious tricks such as pushing us to avoid pain and to make our decisions based on what hurts or does not hurt. He correlates lies in our thought-life that match our experiences from the past, deceiving us into listening to him instead of God. Listening to the enemy, the *sark* or avoiding pain can lead to addictions. Our hope is in learning to recognize the enemy's strategies and in learning to recognize God's voice of truth. We must face our pain within loving, joy-filled relationships so that we can walk free from the enemy and addictions. James 4:7 tells us, "Resist the devil and he will flee from you." John 8:32 admonishes us: "You shall know the truth and the truth shall make you free."

---

[32] The source for this quote is lost to me. Perhaps it can be found on www.lifetime.org

SECTION III—ADDITIONAL SUMMARIES

CHAPTER TEN: SUMMARIES OF THE BRAIN LEVELS AND PROCESSING PAIN

Goal: to further understand the brain levels and how healing from emotional pain fits each level.

INTRODUCTION

As I have done this study on how the brain science fits with relating, my small groups have found it helpful to see the brain levels in different formats. The terms are new and the concepts take some time and study to grasp. You may even be wondering why it matters to know the levels and how they fit with emotional pain. That is a good question. The answer is important.

Emotional pain feels different in each level and what we need for interventions and solutions are different according to how we are feeling. Knowing what is going on with our pain can help us better discover how to receive healing and get our relationships back on track. It is not necessary to memorize all the functions and differences, but a good understanding can help us when there are bumps and conflict and pain. It can help us know what others need when we see them in pain.

185

When using this material in my small groups, we have used three different formats, besides the basics in Chapter Two, to look at how the brain science and healing and growing fit together. Here is one in the form of a chart. In order for the print not to be too small, the chart is divided into two sections:

Brain Levels and Functions

THRIVING	NOT THRIVING	BRAIN LEVEL	FUNCTIONS
Level 1) Belonging	Insecure Attachment	The Attachment Center (Thalamus) **Who or what is important to me?**	Bonding, attaching, who or what is important to me, belonging, draw close or be alone
Level 2) Receiving & giving life.	Self-centered	The Evaluation Center (Amygdala) **What is Good, Bad, Scary?**	Evaluate good, bad, scary, approach or avoid, life giving or not, warns to flee or fight.
Level 3) Synchronizing, Return-to-joy, Forgiveness	Loss of Synchronization	The "Mother Core" (Cingulate) **Peace, Joy, Distress**	Learns personal space, tracks eye movements, dance, empathy, true joy, synchronizes upper and lower brain levels, detects lying, downloads to others, synchs joy & quiet, returning to joy from distress
Level 4) Maturity	Immaturity	The Joy Center (Pre-frontal-cortex) **My identity and attention to the World**	3 way focus, calms level 2, focus attention, impulse control, goal directed behavior, functions for relating well, creativity, personal identity, moral and social behavior
Level 5) Knowing My Heart	Living by the Flesh	The Logic Center (Left and Right Hemispheres together) **My explanations of my life**	Language, storytelling, logic, reasoning, explaining, words

Brain Levels—Pain and Healing

RESULT WHEN DISTRESSED	PAIN	HEALING NEED	INTERVENTIONS
Level 1) Attachment Pain	I feel alone.	A secure attachment	Immanuel Process, identify &face attachment pain, take pain to a secure person, a secure bond with Jesus, deal with addictions and learn to suffer well
Level 2) Fear & desire to make it stop, fear runs the life	I feel disconnected and afraid.	Someone to keep me emotionally connected in spite of pain & ability to keep a memory conscious	Immanuel Process, need a person with L3 skills with high capacity to move me up the Control Center. Jesus can be the one.
Level 3) Top 2 layers of emotional center shut down. Lose their functions.	I feel overwhelmed.	Someone to be glad to be with me, relational, help me return to joy while I am feeling negative emotions. Big Six.	Someone to synch & help me return to joy. Immanuel Process. Feeling talk, active listening, worship music, dance, face to face communication, 12 Step programs, listen to and tell 4+. Stories about the Big Six. Download from a bigger brain.

Brain Levels—Pain and Healing (cont.)

RESULT WHEN DISTRESSED	PAIN	HEALING NEED	INTERVENTIONS
Level 4) Lose ability to act like myself, lose maturity, goal direction, impulse control, calm, etc.	I've lost who I truly am and feel childish.	To resume acting like myself during intense emotions, see a model of how to act & be satisfied with how I handled a situation.	Immanuel Process, community to help me mature after ID lacks, non-verbal stories, journaling, interactive quieting, remedial aggression w/ a man, joy w/woman, quiet w/woman
Level 5) Shuts down top layers, words are gone, words do not help, cannot explain myself, can't focus well, internal conflict, can't tell a story about my past.	I just do not understand. I feel confused.	I need to make sense of the painful experience, have God's perspective, and information will help.	Immanuel Process, Jesus can help me see how things fit, truth sets me free. Find God in activity or quiet according to my way of responding.

The charts briefly summarize the brain levels, functions and pain processing pathways for those of us who love charts. Another way to look at the levels, functions and pain interventions is through statements I gleaned from the lectures of Dr. Jim Wilder, Ed Khouri and/or Dr. Karl Lehman at the THRIVE Conference in 2009. These statements are thought-provoking and bring about good discussions if used in a group setting. They are divided into the five brain levels and will have some repetition from the charts as they tie together what we studied in earlier chapters, helping us better understand how the brain processes pain, how the process brings healing and how joy-filled relationships make a difference.

CONDENSED THRIVE NOTES 2009

Level 1 (**Attachment**) I need a secure bond. Bonds form our reality.

How well we synchronize at Level 3, the bonds we had at Level 1 in early life, leaves the most enduring pattern in our personality. On one end, we will show no importance to feelings (dismissive), on the other, we will feel hurt all the time and think about nothing but feelings (distracted) or on the other end we will be afraid of the very people we need (disorganized). These feelings distort our reality but feel real to us at the time we are feeling them.

When in Level 1 pain, all hurts. I feel alone. We call this **Attachment Pain. (See next section.)** Helpers need to notice the person's type of bond. Notice if there was failure to thrive.

If I'm in pain and get no response from a person, I will turn to other pleasures. I misinterpret things and intensify things. In order to repair I need a current secure bond and a joyful community.

Bonds are more important than healing. We want to be seen and loved as a person, not a project.

Relationships are more important than problems. Staying relational is more important than solving problems.

Sometimes it is slow for Jesus to change things because He is making us bond with each other.

We need three-way bonds outside of marriage so two-way bonds won't become a couple (if not married). This can happen with same sex bonds that are not in a community or a third-face bond.

We build new brains by "Rejoicing with those who rejoice and weeping with those who weep."

Interventions: Immanuel Process, Identify Attachment Pain (AP-see below), a secure bond with Jesus, take my pain to a secure person. Face AP, deal with addictions and learn to suffer well.

ATTACHMENT PAIN & THE NUCLEUS ACCUMBENS: We need to teach people about Attachment Pain (AP). It is not a well-known topic and is the underlying cause for many problems, especially addictions.

If I avoid AP I will use BEEPS to medicate the pain. (**B**ehaviors, **E**vents, **E**xperiences, **P**eople, **S**ubstances)[33]

Joy and AP strongly influence pre-conscious decisions of what I will notice. New bonds, such as falling in love, change my reality.

AP is the deepest level of pain, when we do not feel like we belong.

---

[33] Ed Khouri, *Restarting*, Shepherd's House, Inc., Pasadena, CA, 2007, page 28

© 2012 Barbara Moon

AP is hidden and powerful. It is the main reason the Relational Circuits (RC's) shut down.

AP makes other pains worse, makes problems feel bigger; we blast others. We will do anything to make AP go away until we get healing and learn to suffer well.

We can't hope to be "loved out of AP," or hope to love others out of AP. Both are toxic hope. Others can only give us enough strength to feel and acknowledge AP and learn to suffer well. Only God can heal it.

Learn to identify AP and re-engage my Relational Circuits. Then I can stop feeding the cravings.

Secure parenting does not produce AP because synchronizing with pain brings validation and comfort.

When there is no synchronizing, no validation and comfort, a child feels great pain. The child will turn to something to dull the pain. Whatever that is will become a habit that turns into an addiction. When older, the cravings will replace relationships. Eventually the craving itself will bring AP. (Khouri[34])

Don't underestimate the power of AP.

AP is felt in the form of cravings—what we think will make us feel better or less distressed. When the RC's are off, we don't realize that what we are craving is belonging—a relationship of joy and peace.[35]

---

[34] Ed Khouri, *Restarting*, Shepherd's House, Inc., Pasadena, CA, 2007, pages 28,
[35] Ed Khouri, *Restarting*, Shepherd's House, Inc., Pasadena, CA, 2007, pages 55-56

When we experience no relationship we will turn to chemicals. Turn to Jesus instead. People who do recovery in relationships get better.

Attachment-pain induced addictions come from an untamed nucleus accumbens (NA), another part of the Attachment Center (Level 1). The nucleus accumbens is the pleasure center in the brain that loudly tells us, "I must have this or I will surely die," while subconsciously using that desired pleasure to dull the pain of unmet closeness. We see an example of an untamed nucleus accumbens in the story of Jacob and Esau in Genesis 25:32. I need to learn to notice what the NA is telling me that I might die if I don't get. Am I thirsty but eating? Am I wanting to connect with someone, but drinking?

Relationship and closeness are what we are really looking for. If accustomed to avoiding pain, the person might not even be aware that pain is there. He just goes after the addictive pleasure. It is vital during the early years to help our children feel emotional pain while being comforted, so that they will not develop habits of avoiding the pain. We must teach them, "You will not surely die." If a child has no place to turn for comfort during his or her emotional pain, his nucleus accumbens will scream for something to cover the pain, something that brings pleasure. That is the beginning of an addiction that will only grow worse as the child matures. (NA ideas from Wilder, *Living With Men*, taken from *Handbook to Joy-Filled Parenting, pp. 149-151)*

Taming the NA is part of learning to do hard things in the Child Stage of maturity. Tame it before puberty by being there to synchronize, calm, comfort and return to joy when upset occurs so that the child will know that "pain means comfort is on the way," instead of learning that pain is something to avoid. Children must be good at producing joy and calming themselves so that they know how to survive the scream of the nucleus accumbens and be able turn off their brain circuits that set it screaming. (pp. 81-83 *Living With Men,* taken from *Handbook to Joy-Filled Parenting, pp. 149-151*)

Level 2 (**Evaluation** of what to approach or avoid) We attach to what makes us feel safe. When feeling unsafe, I need someone with a high capacity mind to sit with me and not de-synchronize so I can deal with fear and either calm or stay connected to a memory in order to process it.

I can de-synchronize to Level 2 from lack of joy capacity or from low capacity caused by stress "under the curve." Under-the-curve stress is consistent stress, stretched over a period of time and may not be easily noticed. (From a lecture by Dr. Karl Lehman)[36]

If there is no synchronization/mutual mind with someone at Level 3, Level 2 will shut down the rest of my brain. I feel disconnected and afraid.

If my brain is trained, I can self-quiet. If it is not, I can't self-quiet.

At Level 2, I can reverse good to think it is bad or scary, and vice versa.

Level 2 can only be influenced indirectly. Words do not help.

---

[36] An example of stress "under the curve" would be living with a person who constantly badgers, controls or demeans. It comes to feel "normal."

In Level 2 pain, all of life is about fear. If I fear receiving, it appears I am falsely mature. If I fear giving, I am a consumer.

A fear-based family or person is *avoiding* one of the Big 6 emotions.

A fear-driven family or person is *afraid* of one of the Big 6.

If I fear Attachment Pain, I will not allow someone else to be alone and hurt; I will try to fix them. I will over nurture and call it mercy. I will manipulate relationships, control, and/or sexualize relationships in order to avoid pain.

I will talk about the other person as the problem.

I will either have a tiny comfort zone or a huge one. Nothing, or everything, is bad. I will have massive fear bonds, reactive anger. I will be results-oriented and not desire-driven. I might be dissociative.

Interventions: I need the Immanuel Process. I need a person who has Level 3 skills with high capacity to help me stay connected and move me up the control center. Jesus can be the one.

I can learn to recognize when my RC's are off. I can ask or be asked, "What do you want?" I can move or be helped to move to sadness and to notice my body which gets Level 4 on.

Level 3 (Relational/Synchronizing) I need someone who has the capacity to sit with me, share my distress and help me return to joy.

I need a mutual mind. That is the same as someone synchronizing with me. This is a learned skill.

Depending on my capacity, I can handle things I have learned to handle, but need help when something new comes along.

I can learn to notice when I am listening to Memorex (Lehman)—my past that is intruding into the present. The main clue is that the feelings are too big for the current situation. This Memorex occurs because I had no synchronization (validation and comfort) in this situation in the past. That was very painful and left me stuck in a "trauma."

If having trouble relating, I need help with mind sight—the ability to understand another's mind. I learn this by listening—and with the help of someone who has good mind sight, someone who can synchronize and return to joy.

I need a third face to repair faulty mind sight if I am believing something wrong about you.

I can tell 4+ Stories about times when I did not have good mind sight. I can look at how my parents did mind sight and how they handled shame. (See Chapter Seven for more on shame)

A narcissist is someone who does not know how to return to joy from shame. They can't handle shame. Their attitude is, "I won't love you unless you love me well enough." They use humiliation (anger and shame at the same time) to get compliance.

If there is no one to sit with me and synchronize and return to joy I will turn to chemicals. I will believe I am bad. I will be scared of my emotions. I will develop addictions that turn off the pain by medicating the nucleus accumbens.

The nucleus accumbens is the pleasure center. It can only feel either pain or pleasure, not both at the same time.

Interventions: Feeling-talk, active listening, worship, music, dance, face to face communication, 12 step programs. Someone to synchronize and help me return to joy. Listen to and tell 4+ Stories about the Big 6 emotions. Download from a bigger brain (a person with a bigger Level 3).

Level 4 (**Joy and Identity Center**) If I did not get what I needed and/or had traumas growing up, I am stuck in the maturing process and need an example of what it is like me to do and to know how to handle things in a satisfying manner.

I can re-enter a situation and, while feeling the feelings, I can imagine how I could have handled it satisfactorily. This is a good thing to do if/when I am beating up on myself.

The painful memory is fully processed through Level 4 when I can answer the question "What is like me and my people to do here?"

When Level 4 is off, I will act reactive, feel hopeless, my timing will be off and I'll have no joy. I will not know how I am affecting you. I will be a loner, have victim mentality, be over responsible, a workaholic, and focus on what I am not, or do the opposite of what others want. I won't notice facial changes and I will not learn from painful consequences. In other words, I will act immaturely.

I will be disorganized in my thinking and not see the least damaging solution. I will have an insatiable desire to be understood.

Trying to reason with me will make it worse. I feel like I have lost who I am.

I need an example or a model of what to do and how to act.

Intervention: Immanuel Process, community help to mature after identifying lacks, Level 4 non-verbal stories, journaling, art therapy, Interactive quieting/remediation of aggression with a man—(retrain from lack of tickle games, wrestling, "I'm gonna get you" games, and learning when to stop aggression. This training should have been done at 12-18 months by Dad.) Build joy with a woman; learn to quiet with a woman. Take-a-breather exercises.

Level 4+/5 (Logic and Language) I need for who I am to fit who I think I am. I need to make sense of my painful experiences and fit them into my worldview. I need to understand what is going on.

When Level 5 is off, I will live from a false self and be inconsistent. I will have to be right; I will accuse and blame, feel confused and anxious and worry. I will just want facts, be unreasonable and contemptuous.

I need help finding out what is weak in my relating skills and what is missing from my brain training and maturity. I feel confused.

I can use staying in Level 5 to avoid pain by trying to analyze instead of feeling.

There is place in the brain that Dr. Lehman calls the Verbal Logical Explainer. The VLE's job is to come up with explanations that help us organize and make sense out of our experiences. If the data it starts with is valid, the explanations will be basically valid. If the data is coming from a triggered place from my past, it will make up explanations based on that data and the explanations will not be valid.

Truth is important because Level 5, the Left Hemisphere, can help me find solutions for the Right Hemisphere when it is in trouble. It can help me realize I am listening to Memorex. It can direct me towards Immanuel Process. It can help me remember the good memories with Jesus.

I need both truth and emotional healing, not just truth. My emotions and actions reveal what I truly believe. I need to face my erroneous beliefs and not run away. Even though something feels true, I can override it with what I know is true when the brain is synchronized and I can suffer well.

Some people think and sort their way through relationships. They rely on predicting others' behaviors according to categories and roles. They want us to help them sort better, explain missed predictions, enforce compliance to expectations, increase their power to get others to behave predictably. This brings about condemnation, judgment, comparing, entitlement, punishing, withdrawing, un-forgiveness, and *sark* based living.

We help people who live by roles and sorting by having no fear bonds with them and engaging Level 4—helping them see what is like us to do and what is satisfying. (See Chapter Eleven for what satisfies). They need a good example. We are not designed for fear-based thinking.

We must learn to see with our heart and the way God sees.

Interventions: Immanuel Process—Jesus can help me see how things fit. Truth sets me free. If I am a sympathetic (activity oriented) responder, find God in something active such as walking. If a parasympathetic (calm/quiet oriented) responder, I can find Him in the quiet, sitting still.

I can make lists of my maturity lacks, list all A and B traumas, observe the right side of my brain, identify bad mind sight, recognize faulty repair methods, learn to live with my limitations, give up toxic hopes. Be able to suffer well when I know what it is like me to do when bad things happen. That is what the brain is looking for. Find lies that bump me. The brain does not tolerate lies well.

Recognize when the Right Hemisphere is stirred up. Journal about the distress; find words. Notice when the past is intruding in the present. Do Immanuel prayer with Jesus. Tell 4+ stories. If you put something into a story, Level 5 will take that and try to organize and fill in the blanks. Use some non-verbal communication.

Identify heart values from suffering **(See Exercise for Chapter One, Dyad Discussion 2).** Stop living by the *sark*, identify my maturity levels. Identify my attachment styles, identify where my brain is stuck.

ANOTHER SUMMARY: JESUS AND THE BRAIN LEVELS

(Summary from an article by Dr. Karl Lehman)

These first two summaries of the brain levels are different but helpful to our understanding and grasp of how the brain science works in relationships. There is one other way that we can look at the brain levels and pain by bringing in the Immanuel Process for healing.

JESUS AND THE BRAIN LEVELS

Level 1 (Attachment Center)   **Pain** (I feel alone) **Healing Need** (A secure attachment)

Jesus is the perfect source of secure attachment. He is always present. He loves me with perfect love and is always glad to be with me.   He never gets triggered, overwhelmed, judgmental or contemptuous. He is perfectly safe. When I can perceive His presence, I will have a secure attachment context in which to process painful experiences and memories.

Level 2 (Evaluation Center)   **Pain** (I feel disconnected and afraid)   **Healing Need** (Someone to keep me emotionally connected in spite of the pain, and the ability to keep the memory conscious)

Jesus is the ideal source for "mutual mind" capacity. He loves me perfectly, He is always glad to be with me even in my pain. He is beyond elder maturity and has infinite capacity, se He is always able to stay with me no matter how intense the pain or how long it might last. To the extent I am able to perceive His presence; I will have a "mutual mind" connection to aid my capacity.

Level 3 (Relational/Synchronizing Center)   **Pain** (I feel overwhelmed)   **Healing Need** (Someone to be glad to be with

© 2012 Barbara Moon

me/return to joy with me [be relational] *while* I am feeling negative emotions—the Big Six)

Jesus is the best source of voluntary capacity *[the possibility of choosing to stay in a memory]* and staying relational. He is always present and always glad to be with us even in pain. He has infinite capacity to stay with us, no matter the experience. He is the ultimate master of maturity skills, able to initiate connection and helps us regain joy and self-relationship. To the extent I can perceive His presence and connect with Him and synchronize with Him, we will have the best possible relational connection to aid my voluntary capacity and Level 3 skills.

Level 4 (Joy and Identity Center) **Pain** (I've lost who I truly am) **Healing Need** (To act like my true self during intense emotions, see a model of how to act if needed, and be satisfied with how I handled the situation)

Jesus is the best source of Level 4 capacity and skill enhancement. He is always present, His maturity is complete and His capacity infinite. He can perfectly model what I need to know/do to handle the situation should I ever encounter it again. To the extent I am able to perceive the Lord's presence, observe Him and follow His example, I will have the best help for level 4 maturity skills.

Level 5 (Logical, Lingual)   **Pain** (I just don't understand)
Healing Need (I need to make sense of the painful experience *[from God's perspective]* and information will help)

Jesus is always with me, always glad to be with me. He offers relationship and has the capacity to stay with me. Jesus is the Truth and the Word by whom all things were created, so he has enough Level 5 skill to help me process and make sense out of my experience. He provides brilliant, elegant perfectly nuanced explanations. To the extent we are able to perceive the Lord's presence and synchronize with Him, we will have the best possible aid for our voluntary capacity and our level 5 skills.

© 2012 Barbara Moon

CHAPTER ELEVEN: REVISITING MATURITY—WHAT SATISFIES?

Goal: to understand the importance of knowing what satisfies.

INTRODUCTION

In his book, *Living with Men*, Dr. Wilder speaks at length of the importance of understanding what satisfies. I have summarized these thoughts into a series of statements that can be very helpful to go through, discuss and grasp. They make a great class discussion when read aloud and discussed. Learning satisfaction is at the heart of correcting maturity problems.

THOUGHTS ON WHAT SATISFIES

1. Knowing what satisfies is a child task. The infant must learn to receive so the child can learn when it is most satisfying to give. *Giving and receiving life is what satisfies.* Maturity is a developing pattern of giving and receiving. It takes both. If I only give, I will stay stuck; if I only receive I will stay stuck. Neither will satisfy.

2. If I am all consuming or all giving, afraid to ask for what I need, I'll never learn to receive and give joyfully and freely.

3. If a child is made to sacrifice too early it will breed dissatisfaction. He may give and give, but not be satisfied. (Learning to share is a hard thing, not sacrificial.)

4. If I don't complete the infant tasks, I will give out of guilt and shame or fear. I will feel guilt or shame when someone wants to give to me. I will try to please.

5. Three things that satisfy must be renewed daily—food, affection, and efforts. (Ecclesiastes 8:15)

6. Learning satisfaction is at the heart of correcting maturity problems.

7. Everyone over the age of four should be discussing satisfaction. It's part of learning from failures.

8. Tell stories of what satisfied you—daily. Ask questions about satisfaction, about all things, whether good or bad.

9. Satisfaction can be small things like which dressing do I want on my salad? Which shirt would go best at this event?

10. When beginning to learn this, at the end of the day look at, "Was this or that satisfying or not." Then begin to categorize what was most or less satisfying. Plan something satisfying for the next day.

11. Learn satisfaction about how I deal with Attachment Pain and the Big Six emotions.

12. When I learn how to regulate feelings, how to do hard things and learn what truly satisfies, I will be ready to be an adult. Learning the adult tasks is a big job.

13. It is not pride to be satisfied with how I handled something.

14.	If I am doing all the giving (enabling), I will have to stop for the other to learn what satisfies. If I am the one doing all the receiving (never grew up), I will have to go through pain lab (learn to feel my negative feelings) and learn to stop avoiding pain. I will need someone to join me in the pain and help me return to joy.
15.	Doing hard things is the simplest form of pain. Learning to be satisfied with doing hard things leads to learning to suffer well. Suffering well leads in turn to learning how to protect others from myself (an adult task).
16.	To learn to suffer well I will need a community who can be wise enough to give just enough help without enabling. They must not be afraid of or indifferent to my pain.
17.	Part of learning to suffer well is learning to deal with the Big Six emotions. I will need a bigger brain to help train mine.
18.	Fear of doing hard things is mostly about feeling hard emotions.
19.	Knowing about maturity is part of seeing the big picture and will help people on their journey to maturity.

SUMMARY

Learning what satisfies is very important for growth in maturity. Satisfaction is something we should be talking about and practicing daily. Sacrificing too young is not satisfying. If we do not know what satisfies, we will give too much or take too much. We need to learn to do hard things before moving to the adult tasks, and feeling hard emotions is one of the hard things. Learning to do hard things is a simple form of pain and will lead to being able to suffer well and not avoid pain. We will need others to help us learn the child tasks and help us practice what satisfies.

CHAPTER TWELVE: THE NINETEEN RELATIONAL SKILLS FOR THRIVING

Goal: to have a concise, Biblical list of the brain skills

INTRODUCTION

The following list of skills for thriving was compiled by Dr. James Wilder and Chris Coursey for the THRIVE conferences presented by www.thrivetoday.org. I have added the definitions and verses. We have covered these nineteen skills here in our study. Keep them in mind and review them as your joy-filled relationships grow. Used with permission.

THE NINETEEN SKILLS FOR THRIVING:

BUILD AND SHARE JOY

I know how to build joy with others of all ages and am progressing with knowing how to keep my own joy bucket full.

"Then he said to them, 'Go, eat of the fat, drink of the sweet, and send portions to him who has nothing prepared; for this day is holy to our Lord. Do not be grieved, for the joy of the LORD is your strength.'"(Nehemiah 8:10)

QUIET MYSELF

I know how to quiet myself in distress and when to ask for help if I am unable to do so.

"Surely I have composed and quieted my soul; Like a weaned child rests against his mother; My soul is like a weaned child within me." (Psalm 131:2)

BONDS FOR TWO

If I did not have strong bonds with my parents, I now have two strong and secure bonds for life. I know how to bond securely with others by moving closer or farther apart at moments that satisfy us both. This is part of synchronizing.

"Now it came about when he had finished speaking to Saul that the soul of Jonathan was knit to the soul of David, and Jonathan loved him as himself." (I Samuel 18:1)

CREATE APPRECIATION

I know how to appreciate others and create feelings of appreciation in others, in order to create closeness and relieve stress.

"So, as those who have been chosen of God, holy and beloved, put on a heart of compassion, kindness, humility, gentleness and patience; bearing with one another, and forgiving each other, whoever has a complaint against anyone; just as the Lord forgave you, so also should you." (Colossians 3: 12, 13)

FAMILY BONDS

I have a place that I can call my community where I am bonded with at least three faces. My community helps me with relating well.

"And if one can overpower him who is alone, two can resist him. A cord of three strands is not quickly torn apart." (Ecclesiastes 4:12)

"Therefore, laying aside falsehood, speak truth each one of you with his neighbor, for we are members of one another." (Ephesians 4:25)

IDENTIFY MY HEART VALUES FROM SUFFERING

I am learning to look at suffering as an opportunity to see what is very important to me because it causes me pain. Doing this will turn a negative into a positive.

"But if we are afflicted, it is for your comfort and salvation; or if we are comforted, it is for your comfort, which is effective in the patient enduring of the same sufferings which we also suffer..." (2 Corinthians 1:6)

FOUR+ STORY TELLING

I am able to tell a coherent story about events in my life while showing the appropriate emotions on my face. This is a sign that my whole brain is synchronized.

"...I myself might have confidence even in the flesh. If anyone else has a mind to put confidence in the flesh, I far more: circumcised the eighth day, of the nation of Israel, of the tribe of Benjamin, a Hebrew of Hebrews; as to the Law, a Pharisee; as to zeal, a persecutor of the church; as to the righteousness which is in the Law, found blameless. But whatever things were gain to me, those things I have counted as loss for the sake of Christ. More than that, I count all things to be loss in view of the surpassing value of knowing Christ Jesus my Lord, for whom I have suffered the loss of all things, and count them but rubbish so that I may gain Christ, and may be found in Him, not having a righteousness of my own derived from the Law, but that which is through faith in Christ, the righteousness which comes from God on the basis of faith, that I may know Him and the power of His resurrection and the fellowship of His sufferings, being conformed to His death; in order that I may attain to the resurrection from the dead. Not that I have already obtained it or have already (become perfect, but I press on so that I may lay hold of that for which also I was laid hold of by Christ Jesus. Brethren, I do not regard myself as having laid hold of it yet; but one thing I do: forgetting what lies behind and reaching forward to what lies ahead, I press on toward the goal for the prize of the upward call of God in Christ Jesus." (Philippians 3:4-14)

IDENTIFY MATURITY LEVELS

When I understand the maturity levels I can discern if I am reacting to a current issue or if I need some healing in an area. I can understand where others are coming from as well.

". . . Until we all attain to the unity of the faith, and of the knowledge of the Son of God, to a mature man, to the measure of the stature which belongs to the fullness of Christ." (Ephesians 4:13)

"For this reason also, since the day we heard of it, we have not ceased to pray for you and to ask that you may be filled with the knowledge of His will in all spiritual wisdom and understanding, so that you will walk in a manner worthy of the Lord, to please Him in all respects, bearing fruit in every good work and increasing in the knowledge of God; strengthened with all power, according to His glorious might, for the attaining of all steadfastness and patience; joyously giving thanks to the Father, who has qualified us to share in the inheritance of the saints in Light." (Colossians 1: 9-12)

TAKE A BREATHER

I know how and when to disengage and allow others to rest when they are tired and before they become overwhelmed. This can take only seconds and is rewarded with trust and love.

"Set a guard, O LORD, over my mouth; Keep watch over the door of my lips. (Psalm 141:3)

TELL NON-VERBAL STORIES

I know how to use timing, tone, facial expressions and body language to communicate and resolve conflicts. This helps develop good emotional and relational capacity.

"As in water face reflects face, so the heart of man reflects man." (Proverbs 27:19)

RETURN TO JOY FROM THE BIG SIX EMOTIONS

I know the Big Six emotions and how well I handle each. I understand how to quiet distress and repair breaks in relationships quickly so the upset will not last long.

"Therefore, laying aside falsehood, SPEAK TRUTH EACH ONE of you WITH HIS NEIGHBOR, for we are members of one another. BE ANGRY, AND yet DO NOT SIN; do not let the sun go down on your anger, and do not give the devil an opportunity. He who steals must steal no longer; but rather he must labor, performing with his own hands what is good, so that he will have something to share with one who has need. Let no unwholesome word proceed from your mouth, but only such a word as is good for edification according to the need of the moment, so that it will give grace to those who hear. Do not grieve the Holy Spirit of God, by whom you were sealed for the day of redemption. Let all bitterness and wrath and anger and clamor and slander be put away from you, along with all malice. Be kind to one another, tender-hearted, forgiving each other, just as God in Christ also has forgiven you." (Ephesians 4: 25-32)

ACT LIKE MYSELF IN THE BIG SIX EMOTIONS

I am able to act the same with others whether we are in joy together or one of us is feeling upset by one of the Big Six emotions. I do not want to damage or withdraw from a relationship I value.

(From the cross) "When Jesus then saw His mother, and the disciple whom He loved standing nearby, He said to His mother, 'Woman, behold, your son!' Then He said to the disciple, 'Behold, your mother!' From that hour the disciple took her into his own household. (John 19:26-27)

HEARTSIGHT

I am able to look at myself, others and circumstances through God's eyes instead of only seeing what went wrong. I can see people's purpose as more important than their malfunction.

". . . while we look not at the things which are seen, but at the things which are not seen; for the things which are seen are temporal, but the things which are not seen are eternal." (2 Corinthians 4:18)

"But the LORD said to Samuel, 'Do not look at his appearance or at the height of his stature, because I have rejected him; for God sees not as man sees, for man looks at the outward appearance, but the LORD looks at the heart.'" (1 Samuel 16:7)

STOP THE *SARK*

The Greek word sark *or* sarx *refers to seeing life according to our own understanding. Thinking I can figure out the right thing to do or be, without God, according to how looks or feels, is the opposite of living from my heart. Living from the* sark *brings blame, accusations, condemnation, resentment, legalism, and other negatives into our relationships, steeping us in lies.*

"Trust in the LORD with all your heart, and do not lean on your own understanding." (Proverbs 3:5)

"But I say, walk by the Spirit, and you will not carry out the desire of the flesh." (Galatians 5:16)

QUIET INTERACTIVELY

I am able to watch for facial cues that will alert me when someone is about to go over the top and I will be able to keep the energy high and fun without going into overwhelm. (Example: Knowing when to stop tickling.)

"As in water face reflects face, so the heart of man reflects man." (Proverbs 27:19)

RECOGNIZE HIGH AND LOW ENERGY RESPONSE STYLES

I am able to recognize and synchronize with which way another person (or myself) is likely to respond to distress. Will they respond with high energy like anger or low energy such as withdrawing?

"Bear one another's burdens, and thereby fulfill the law of Christ." (Galatians 6:2)

IDENTIFY ATTACHMENT STYLES

I know the four attachment styles, the principle one that I have and how they affect me, as well as how they affect others. I understand how the insecure attachments affect relationships and emotions. The dismissive style underestimates feelings and relationships; distracted leads to exaggeration of hurts and needs; disorganized makes one afraid to get close to those he loves and needs.

"Now we who are strong ought to bear the weaknesses of those without strength and not just please ourselves. Each of us is to please his neighbor for his good, to his edification. For even Christ did not please Himself; but as it is written, 'The reproaches of those who reproached you fell on Me.' For whatever was written in earlier times was written for our instruction, so that through perseverance and the encouragement of the Scriptures we might have hope. Now may the God who gives perseverance and encouragement grant you to be of the same mind with one another according to Christ Jesus..." (Romans 15:1-5)

INTERVENE WHERE THE BRAIN IS STUCK OR DE-SYNCHRONIZED

I know when someone is about to fall apart and de-synchronize. I know the five levels of pain associated with a de-synchronized brain and this will help me find a solution to the pain.

"But the wisdom from above is first pure, then peaceable, gentle, reasonable, full of mercy and good fruits, unwavering, without hypocrisy. (James 3:17)

"Therefore, confess your sins to one another, and pray for one another so that you may be healed. The effective prayer of a righteous man can accomplish much. (James 5:16)

RECOVER FROM COMPLEX EMOTIONS

When I know how to return to joy from the Big Six one at a time, I can work on returning to joy and quiet when they are combined.

"Out of the depths I have cried to You, O LORD. Lord, hear my voice! Let Your ears be attentive to the voice of my supplications. If You, LORD, should mark iniquities, O Lord, who could stand? But there is forgiveness with You, that You may be feared. I wait for the LORD, my soul does wait. And in His word do I hope. My soul waits for the Lord More than the watchmen for the morning; indeed, more than the watchmen for the morning. Israel, hope in the LORD; for with the LORD there is loving kindness, and with Him is abundant redemption. And He will redeem Israel from all his iniquities. (Psalm 130 and many others)

SUMMARY

The nineteen skills can serve as a concise list of joy-filled relationship skills. Keep them handy for reference as you work through the chapters and exercises. Spread joy and Immanuel healing through your family and community. May you heal and grow and enjoy all that God has for His children.

APPENDIX: STUDY QUESTIONS AND EXERCISES

In this section, you will find study questions and exercises for each chapter. Some of these exercises and suggestions were compiled by Dr. Jim Wilder and Chris and Jen Coursey who run the THRIVE conference training that I have attended.

THRIVE exercises are used by permission of Chris and Jen Coursey. For more information on THRIVE training, THRIVE exercises or THRIVE products please visit www.thrivetoday.org and www.lifemodel.org

For more exercises purchase a THRIVE Conference Skill Guide at www.thrivetoday.org

Note: The exercises here have been designed to be done with bonded partners, such as family members, OR within groups of three or more people. They are not designed to build "couple bonds" between two people who are not married. When not done this way, there is a danger that some exercises could become "sexualized."[37] This is not a danger within a group setting. Bonded pairs can do them at home. It is okay to do them with children when age appropriate.

---

[37] Ed Khouri, *Restarting Workbook*, page171

CHAPTER ONE: MATURITY

1. Discuss the goal for maturity.
2. Have you recognized where you are lacking in any needs or tasks?
3. What do the maturity levels say about someone's value?
4. What are some ingredients for maturing?
5. Whose job is it to help others mature? Whose job is it not?
6. Discuss the following tips about maturity and how they apply to your life:

- If someone gets upset when they receive a "no," this is Child maturity.
- During conflict an Infant/adult will take care of #1 (Self). (Adults can take care of more than one person at a time.)
- During conflict a Child/adult will take sides. (Adults satisfy all and compromise.)
- An Adult will protect others from him or herself by disengaging in order to not harm.
- A Child only does what he feels like doing until about age 5. You have to change his feelings about the topic to get co-operation.
- A Parent serves without expecting anything in return.
- An Adult/teenager knows the big picture and that choices & actions affect history.

EXERCISES: In order to grow more comfortable with some of the exercises that require eye-to-eye contact, we will begin with an easy one.

DYAD DISSCUSSION 1: A story of us. Sit with your spouse or a close friend. Sit "knee to knee" so you can look at each other's eyes. You are going to take turns telling a "story of us," which is a positive, fun, joyful, or touching story about the two of you. *If you are in a group of people* who do not know each other well, sit with someone and tell a story about yourself that is a story about something that brought you joy. It can be from any time in your life. Either way, one person will talk and the other will listen without interrupting. Then switch for the other to talk while you listen.

DYAD DISCUSSION 2: What is the main characteristic of my heart? "Knee to knee," tell your partner what you think is the main characteristic of your heart. (If your group is very small, you can do this as a group.) What is "really like you?" (This may not be the way you act when upset.) If this is difficult, here are some questions to help you know your heart: How do I want others to see me? What do I want people to say about me at my funeral? What causes me pain? (What causes us pain shows us our heart by looking at what is *opposite* of what causes the pain.) For example: If you are really hurt by betrayal—then you are very loyal. If dishonesty hurts you, then you are honest. If meanness hurts you, then you are kind, etc. Let your partner help you know your heart. When you have come up with 1-3 characteristics, let the other person have a turn.

Knowing the characteristics of your heart helps turn negatives into positives, because most people think pain is bad; therefore, whatever causes you pain, you avoid and think is bad. The enemy wants us to stop doing the things that are from our hearts, so he uses pain to make us stop doing it. Instead, see what the pain is telling you about the heart Jesus gave you.

When you see another person in pain about something they think is bad, help them see the opposite that is the characteristic of their heart.

CHAPTER TWO: INTRODUCTION TO THE TECHNICAL WHYS

1. Go back over the definitions in Chapter Two and evaluate your understanding of the terms now.

EXERCISE: Repeat Dyad Discussion I above with everyone telling a story about something that brought them joy.

CHAPTER THREE: THE NEW BRAIN STUDIES

1. Discuss with your partner whose story you most indentified with—Daniel's, Kaleb's, Jessica's, Veronica's, Vanessa's, or Will's.
2. Why does receiving come before giving?
3. How does it feel to synchronize with another person?
4. What does it feel like when someone does not synchronize with you?
5. What is going on when two people synchronize joy and quiet?
6. What is the "attachment light" in the brain and what does it do?
7. What can help you not fear disconnects (ruptures)?
8. When Level 2 is running the life, what is life based on?

9. How do Level 4 functions help traumas and/or fear?

10. What is "suffering well?" How are you doing with that?

11. What happens when Level 5 and 4 melt down, desynchronize?

EXERCISES: DYAD 1: Building Joy and Synchronizing. Sit knee to knee with your partner. You will look into each other's *left eye* and smile. There is no talking but there might be some giggling. Synchronize with the other's intensity and height of joy. Build the joy higher until recognizing in the other, or sensing in yourself, the need to look away and disengage. It is okay to look away. It is not a staring contest. Disengaging might take only a second or so. Then re-engage and build joy again. You will synchronize joy and quiet, intensity, heart rates, breathing, etc. The more mature brain will go by the other's lead for intensity and amount of joy, disengaging so as not to overwhelm. (This is what we do with babies around that second to third month when they began to smile and interact.)

TRIAD DISCUSSION 2: This exercise will practice the three-way bond. Get into groups of *three* people, sitting close where two can build joy face to face and the third person will be "God" who is observing the other two. As the two build joy, they will glance over at "God" every few seconds to note how "he" is delighting in them building joy together. After about 2 minutes, switch around until each person has had a turn to be "God."

CHAPTER FOUR: BONDING, SYNCHRONIZATION, JOY AND QUIET

© 2012 Barbara Moon

1. Which of the four bonds do you think you had as a young child? What steps do you need to take to improve how you relate to others when their "attachment light" is off or on?
2. How does synchronizing affect each bond?
3. What is the definition of joy? How do we learn and communicate joy?
4. What happens when we do not allow someone to rest after a high state of joy?
5. What benefits come from building joy and quiet together?

EXERCISES: We will repeat the joy-building exercise from Chapter Three. This is one of the most important exercises for re-training the brain.

DYAD 1: Building Joy and Synchronizing. Sit knee to knee with your partner. You will look into each other's left eye and smile. There is no talking but there might be some giggling. Synchronize with the other's intensity and height of joy. Build the joy higher until recognizing in the other, or sensing in yourself, the need to look away and disengage. It is okay to look away. It is not a staring contest. Disengaging might take only a second or so. Then re-engage and build joy again. You will synchronize joy and quiet, intensity, heart rates, breathing, etc. The more mature brain will go by the other's lead for intensity and amount of joy, disengaging so as not to overwhelm.

DYAD 2 Or As A GROUP: Quiet together. Sit quietly together without talking. You can close your eyes. Calm your breathing, calm your mind, relax and sit quietly for 2 minutes. Afterwards, discuss how it felt and if it was difficult to calm yourself or sit quietly. Were you quiet on the outside but not on the inside?

CHAPTER FIVE: RETURN TO JOY

1. What are the definitions of return to joy?
2. What two things have to happen in order to build return-to-joy circuits?
3. Look at the definitions for the Big Six emotions. Which emotion do you have the most trouble with?
4. What does it mean to stay relational and act like oneself in intense emotions?
5. What happens when one does not have a path back from a particular emotion? Which ones do you struggle with? How do you sidetrack or avoid the emotions?
6. What is the key to relationships? Is this part of your life? How can you work on it?
7. What happens in the brain when the level of distress passes the level of the Joy Bucket's capacity?

EXERCISES: For this chapter we are going to learn to tell 4+Stories (Remember 4+ is the same as Level 5). 4+Stories are the key to helping others learn to return to joy from the Big Six. The following guidelines will help you to understand how to tell a 4+ Story.[38] They

---

[38] Used with permission from THRIVE leaders Jen & Chris Coursey, www.thrivetoday.org

are called 4+ Stories because when telling one, all levels of our brain must be synchronized and functioning. You will find an example written out below, although 4+Stories should be told face-to-face.

GUIDELINES FOR TELLING 4+ STORIES

It must be a story you have told before if possible.

It should be of medium intensity level.

You should feel safe to tell it.

Use enough words to take about 3 minutes.

Use feeling words.

You want to evoke the emotion in your listener.

The listener does not talk or interrupt.

The story is about *you*, not someone you know.

Describe how your body felt.

Show the authentic emotion on your face.

State whether you did or did not "act like yourself."

State how it is or would have been "like you" to act during this emotion.

Maintain eye contact during the story telling.

If about returning to joy, tell how you got back to joy from the emotion.

An Example of a 4+Story—Fear: (4+Stories work best when told face to face. I'm putting one here as an example.)

"Several years ago, my family was camping with friends at a nearby lake. The other family had a speedboat that could pull a large inner tube. Bill took his daughter, Kelly, and my daughter, Jodi out on the tube. Bill's son, Billy, and my son, Greg, were in the boat. Both girls were sitting in the hole. My husband and Bill's wife were sitting on the shore which was built up with large rocks covered by chicken wire netting. Bill decided to swing the girls around on the tube, close to the shore so that they could wave at us. As I was watching the boat turn, all of a sudden my heart skipped a beat. Then it started to beat faster. My stomach knotted with terror. I could see by the arc of the rope tying the tube to the boat that the tube was going to hit that wall covered in rocks. I could hardly breathe as I watched the tube head for that wall with two precious girls sitting unaware in the tube. I wanted to close my eyes because I just knew that my daughter's head was going to hit the wall. But I didn't. I was almost frozen.

The tube hit the wall—and bounced off. By this time, Bill had realized what was going to happen. Greg dove into the water before the boat even stopped and I jumped in from the shore. I helped Kelly out of the tube and looked at Jodi. She had a deep cut on her arm and scratches on her leg. I drug the tube over to the shore and the men lifted it out of the water. Jodi was not hurt any other way. The tube had folded up around the girls when it hit the wall.

I acted like myself during this fear because I didn't panic; I remained calm and did what needed to be done. I did not blame Bill at all and I thanked God that the girls were okay. I was glad to be with everyone in the distress. We calmly drove to the ER and Jodi got some stitches in her elbow. God turned this fearful event into a blessing when Bill's insurance paid for the ER after ours already had. Jodi was able to get braces with that money."

DYAD DISCUSSION 1: 4+Return-to-Joy stories. These stories can be told one-on-one or in a group anytime, anywhere, and any age when appropriate. But for now, sit with your partner face to face, but it does not have to be knee to knee. Using the guidelines above for a 4+ story, one of you pick one of the Big Six emotions from Chapter Five and prepare to tell a story about yourself concerning one of the emotions. As you tell the story, following the guidelines, you will help your listener(s) gain or strengthen a path back to joy from that emotion. It is okay if you did not act like yourself in the emotion. You can tell how you *wish* you had acted. If appropriate, tell how you returned to joy. Switch and allow the other person to tell a story with one of the Big Six.

DYAD DISCUSSION 2: Another 4+Story. Pick a different emotion that has not been used and each person tell another story. Remember, no talking while the other is telling their story

CHAPTER SIX: IMMANUEL PROCESS, RELATIONAL CIRCUITS AND TRIGGERING

1. What are Relational Circuits? What happens when they are off?
2. What are some questions to ask Jesus during the Immanuel Process?
3. What five things have to happen for us to process a painful memory?
4. What is appreciation? Do you have at least three appreciation memories?
5. What are you like when your RC's are off?
6. Which of the *Shalom for My Body* exercises is the easiest?[39]
7. Look at the section that details the Immanuel Process. Do you want that to be your lifestyle?
8. What is a trigger and how does knowing about them help you?
9. What is the Verbal Logical Explainer (VLE)?[40]
10. Can you think of a time recently when you were triggered and conflict arose in a relationship?
11. Look at the list that explains how to know that RC's are off. Is it worth memorizing?

EXERCISE I: FINDING AN APPRECIATION MEMORY:
As a group or personally, take a moment to think of something that makes you feel good, makes you want to say, "Ahhhh!" Sit with that feeling for about 15 seconds. Next, *give that memory a one-word*

---

[39] Ed Khouri, *Belonging Workbook*
[40] Dr. Karl Lehman, *Outsmarting Yourself*

name. Go around the group and tell your one-word name. If there is time, give a very brief description of your appreciation moment. For example: "My word is *beach.* I love to be at the beach." If you do appreciation with people you are with all the time, take note of their one-word name. In a kind and calm way, you can remind them of their appreciation memory and it will help them calm. Teach this to your children.

EXERCISE 2: Do each of the three *Shalom for My Body* exercises. After learning them, begin each group time with one of them to be certain that everyone's RC's are on.[41]

EXERCISE 3: Try the Immanuel Process as a group.[42] Do one of the body exercises. Then go to prayer, asking everyone to find Jesus in a good memory or an appreciation memory. Then ask Jesus what He wants each one to know tonight/today? Does He want to heal a painful memory by showing where He was when it happened? Does He want to speak words of delight, encouragement, etc? Sit quietly for about two minutes. Then thank Him and close. Ask if anyone wants to share what they heard. I have seen many healings, during group, in this 3-5 minute period and/or heard testimonies of people hearing God.

EXERCISE 4: 3-3-3 Make this an every-day exercise. Tell 3 people 3 things that you are thankful for about your day **today**. Tell someone 3 things you are thankful for about three different people in your day. Tell someone 3 things you are thankful to God for today. You can mix and match who you tell and how many different things.

---

[41] Ed Khouri, *Belonging Workbook*
[42] Dr. Wilder, Chris Coursey, *Share Immanuel* booklet

CHAPTER SEVEN: REVISITING SHAME—THE REMEDY FOR NARCISSISM

1. What is narcissism and what is its cause?
2. How are our brains wired for joy and shame? What is the purpose of God wiring us for shame?
3. What is the difference in "good" shame and "toxic" shame?
4. What does a good shame message communicate?
5. What is the Hebrew word for what we are calling narcissism? What does it mean?
6. What is the most common response a narcissist gives to a shame message?
7. How can we help a person who has no path back to joy from shame?

EXERCISE: Review the guidelines for telling a 4+Story. See if you can come up with a shame story from your own life. It is all right if you did not act like yourself. Tell the story to a partner or to the group.

An Example of a 4+ Shame Story: "Years ago I attended a conference by a well-known speaker. It was a new experience for me and I was enlightened by the information. At a break, the speaker was sitting at a table by himself, and I went up to talk to him. He did not smile and was very rude and unfriendly. I was shocked. My heart started beating faster, I wanted to run away and the smile disappeared from my face and eyes. I acted like myself because I was not rude back. I did not act like myself because I took that there was something wrong with me that this person would not want to talk to me. I wish I had been able to say something short and true to him about his behavior, but I was not at that kind of place in my journey. I talked to God about my feelings and went on with the conference although I could not "return to joy" with this person."

CHAPTER EIGHT: REVISITING THREE-WAY BONDS—VALIDATION AND COMFORT[43]

1. What is a joyful three-way bond and what are the benefits of a three-way bond?
2. What are the two ingredients that help build a three-way bond?
3. What is validation? What is comfort?
4. Where are some places we can find comfort?
5. What happens when we did not grow a joyful three-way bond or get validation and comfort?
6. What skills and brain functions do we lose when distress overwhelms our level of joy?
7. What are some ways we can get help for our lack of three-way bond, validation and comfort?

EXERCISE: DYAD DISCUSSION: Get with a partner and take turns telling each other a story about a time when you did, or did not, get validated or comforted. How did you feel? If not validated, what do

---

[43] *Belonging Facilitator Workbook*, Ed Khouri, E. James Wilder, Shepherd's House Inc. P.O. Box 40096, Pasadena, CA 91114 pp. 58-61

230   © 2012 Barbara Moon

you wish had happened? Synchronize with your partner. Pray for each other.

CHAPTER NINE: SATAN'S THREE STRATEGIES

1. What are Satan's three strategies to keep us defeated?
2. Which strategy causes you to stumble most often? What steps do you need to take to learn a better way?
3. What are BEEPS?[44] What causes addictions?
4. Do you recognize that you have an addiction to any of these? What steps do you need to take to remedy your addiction?
5. What are some "old tapes" that you hear in your head that are lies from Satan? How are you going to work on replacing the tapes with God's truth?

EXERCISE: DYAD OR TRIAD DISCUSSION: Get in a small group of two or three and discuss what you understand about the three strategies and how they can change your walk with God.

CHAPTER TEN: SUMMARIES OF THE BRAIN LEVELS AND PROCESSING PAIN

1. What is Attachment Pain?
2. How does Attachment Pain affect us?
3. What is the nucleus accumbens and why does it need to be tamed?

---

[44] Ed Khouri, *Restarting*, Shepherd's House, Inc., Pasadena, CA, 2007, pages 28, 44-45 Belo

EXERCISE: Discuss the times that you seem to feel Attachment Pain. What do you do with it? What do you turn to for comfort? Who can help validate and comfort you?

CHAPTER ELEVEN: REVISITING MATURITY—WHAT SATISFIES?

1. Do you know what satisfies?
2. Do you know how to both receive and give? What if we only do one of them?

EXERCISE: DYAD DISCUSSION 1: What brings me satisfaction? Sit knee to knee with your spouse or a close friend. With good eye contact, tell your partner what gives you joy and brings you satisfaction. The other person will listen without interruption. Remember that "receiving and giving life" is what satisfies. Some things that you talk about will be unique to you and others will be more universal. After about 3 minutes, switch and allow the other person to tell you what brings them joy and satisfaction.

DYAD DISCUSSION 2: Telling a 4+ Joy Story. Sit knee to knee with your partner. You are going to take turns telling the other a joyful story. It can be from any time-frame of your life. One will talk; the other will listen. Tell a story about something that brought you joy, using the guidelines above. Then switch. Synchronize with one another as you look at each other's faces and eyes. Show the authentic emotion on your face with the goal of evoking the emotion in your listener. Talk about how your body felt during the event. The story should be about 3 minutes.

RECOMMENDED READING

Share Immanuel Booklet—E. James Wilder, Ph.D. and Chris Coursey, www.thrivetoday.org

Living With Men—E. James Wilder, Ph.D., www.lifemodel.org

Outsmarting Yourself—Dr. Karl Lehman, www.kclehman.com

THRIVING: Recover Your Life—full courses by Ed Khouri, www.lifemodel.org Ed is working on a new name and website

The Life Model: Living from the Heart Jesus Gave You—E. James Wilder, Ph.D, et.al. www.lifemodel.org

Handbook to Joy-Filled Parenting—Barbara Moon, www.lulu.com/barbaramoon www.amazon.com

Jewels for My Journey—Barbara Moon, www.lulu.com/barbaramoon www.amazon.com

Made in the USA
Lexington, KY
08 April 2016